Eve in Ireland

About the Author

Ailish McFadden has worked for decades as an occupational therapist in child and family mental health and related services. Ailish is committed to documenting the lived experiences of Irish women over the last 100 years. She lives in County Kildare.

Eve in Ireland

Controlling and Silencing Irish Women, 1922–1972

Ailish McFadden

The Liffey Press

Published by
The Liffey Press
'Clareville', 307 Clontarf Road
Dublin D03 PO46, Ireland
www.theliffeypress.com

A catalogue record of this book is available from the British Library.

ISBN 978-1-0686645-1-9

Printed in Northern Ireland by W&G Baird

CONTENTS

Special appreciation to Joe, Sarah, Tristan, Alice and P.J. for your endless support.

In honour of Alice Kelly (née McGrane) and all those women born into the opening decades of independent Ireland.

1.

New State, New Life, Old Ways

For many who were born in Ireland and received a Catholic education during the 1900s, memories of the images that surrounded us remain seared in our mind. One abiding memory of the convent classroom includes a crucified Jesus hung on the wall over the dusty blackboard. His dropped head was pierced with a crown of thorns and his blood-stained hands and feet reminded us constantly that he suffered and died a terrible death for our sins.

Over the door was a gold-framed picture of his mother, the Blessed Virgin Mary. Her shoulders draped with a royal-blue

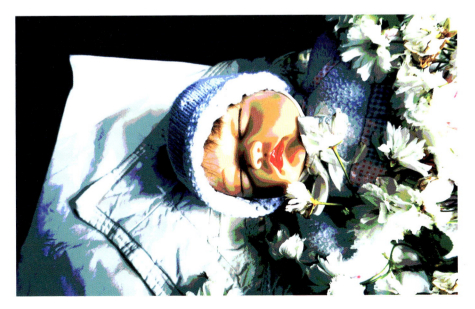

cloak, she stood on a cloud and radiated sunlight as she ascended into heaven. Her serene face reminded us that chastity was honoured above all other virtues.

In the hallway, above the exit door, a framed portrait of Pádraig Pearse was screwed to the wall. His faraway expression and youthful face reminded us that men have died for Ireland, and that some became martyrs. We were taught he was a hero of our nation who led the 1916 Easter Rising, a rebellion that concluded with him, his brother William and others being executed by British forces in the yard at Kilmainham Gaol.

These images were woven into the psyche of generations of Irish children, along with the content of *A Catechism of Catholic Doctrine*. Through this basket-weave of history the children of the Irish Free State were embraced by a church–state alliance, which flourished in a position of isolation from the outside world. While this alliance positively served to create structures for the provision of health and education services in an infantile state, government-commissioned investigations have revealed that these patriarchal structures inflicted profoundly negative impacts on many women and their children, which endure to this day.

Pádraic Pearse

PADRAIC PEARSE (1879-1916) born in Dublin son of an English sculptor. His mother was Margaret Brady from Co. Meath. He was President of the Provisional Government of the Irish Republic, Commandant-General Commander-in-Chief of the army. In this capacity he led the Rising in 1916, and read the Proclamation outside the G.P.O. Dublin. At his Court-martial he said : "If our deed has not been sufficient to win freedom, our children will win it by a better deed.' He was executed in Kilmainham Jail on May 3rd.

Printed in the Republic of Ireland by BADL, Cork

If a generation is marked by the passage of thirty years, today's Irish are just six generations away from the physical and existential crisis resulting from the Famine of the mid-1800s. At that time the levers

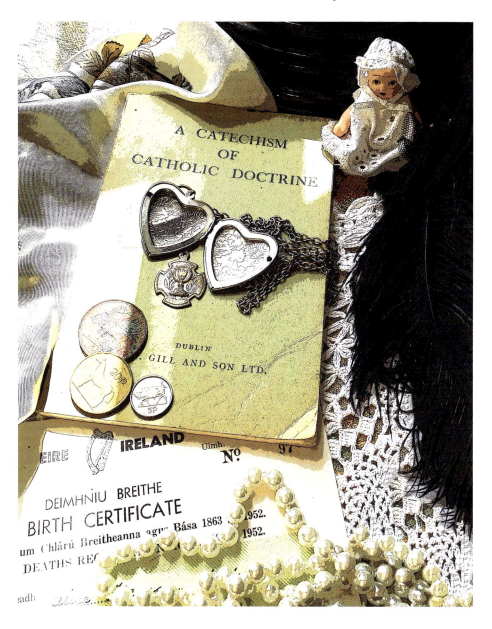

of social and political power, both at local and national level, remained firmly in the grip of the land-owning class – a privileged elite who, over centuries, imposed structures for acquiring and maintaining control of land, wealth and access to power. The titled individuals at the top of this power pyramid were regarded as the aristocracy, who valued links to London and empire.

3

Terence Dooley records in *The Decline and Fall of the Dukes of Leinster, 1872–1948* that:

> Until the last quarter of the nineteenth century, the Irish aristocracy were part of a supra-national British landowning class that controlled most aspects of economic, social and political life at estate, local and national levels. They comprised a tiny minority of around 100 families in a post-Famine population of around 3.5 million people.[1]

This reality contributed to the backdrop for the 1916 Rising and the transformation of Irish political and cultural life in the early decades of the twentieth century.

In *Occasions of Sin*, Diarmaid Ferriter writes:

> The Famine of the 1840s, resulting in the death of over 1 million people and the emigration of over 2 million in the decade 1846–1855, was an event that impacted significantly on Irish sexual behaviour and on marriage and fertility.[2]

The history of women, children and family 'cannot be divorced from the history of other dominant themes in post-Famine Irish history – land, religion and identity, in particular'.[3]

Alexis Guilbride's chapter 'Infanticide: The Crime of Motherhood', in *Motherhood in Ireland*, explores the context for the cultural exclusion of women from opportunities for self-autonomy and power in the decades that followed the establishment of the Irish Free State. Referencing the work of Tom Inglis entitled *Moral Monopoly: The Catholic Church in Modern Irish Society*, Guilbride writes:

> The tenant farmers who had survived the Famine had learned the bitter lesson: the subdivision of small farms was economically unviable. The continuing tradition of

rearing large families to work the land, meant that, where only one son could inherit the land and thus marry, his siblings must remain celibate or leave the country.[4]

These outcomes, which followed years of starvation, emigration and agitation at a local and national level, were to become imprinted on the structure of family life in Ireland. While they may have served to enhance social and political stability, they contributed to gender-based inequality and acceptance of exclusion as a means for maintaining the status quo. As this was to play out in negative and positive ways in the lives of all concerned, the consequences for those who did not conform to community values and expectations proved discriminatory and often traumatic.

Along with the visual images, symbols and doctrine ingrained in Catholic children through schools and home environments during the first fifty years post-1922, there are three men whose lives impacted significantly on our identity and on Ireland's development during the twentieth century. Considered by many to be heroic change-makers, they led the population back to the fundamental touchstones of Irish identity – the Irish language, Roman Catholicism, valuing the family surname and resistance to external influences. These three men were Pádraig Pearse, Éamon de Valera and Archbishop John Charles McQuaid.

As *Eve in Ireland* reflects the lived experience of women during those fifty years, the following content presents a glimpse into the relationship each of these men had with their mothers.

Pádraig Pearse was born to James and Margaret in 1879. James was a stonemason and Margaret came from a traditional Catholic family and is remembered as a pious woman who devoted her life to her four children. 'She was a loving mother and Pádraig was particularly close to her.'[5] When facing the death

penalty following the failed 1916 rebellion, Pádraig penned a poem honouring his mother. Among the words of love and respect, he wrote as if from her heart:

> Lord, thou art hard on mothers;
> We suffer in their coming and their going;
> And tho' I grudge them not, I weary, weary
> Of the long sorrow – And yet I have my joy;
> My sons were faithful, and they fought.[6]

One of Pádraig's comrades was Éamon de Valera. Éamon was an American-born volunteer in the 1916 Rising, who, in the decades that followed went on to become an influential politician, serving first as Taoiseach and then as President of Ireland. In his book *Eamon de Valera*, T. Ryle Dwyer writes of de Valera's early years. Born to Catherine Coll in 1882 in New York, as a small child Éamon was brought to Ireland and was left in the care of his uncle and grandmother. His father, a Spanish immigrant to the United States, died two year after Éamon's birth. In the years that followed his arrival into Ireland, his pleas to return to the USA and his mother were unsuccessful. This experience, along with rumours of his legitimacy, may have contributed to a sense of detachment and lack of belonging.[7]

PRESIDENT DE VALERA

Following the death of his grandmother in 1895, Éamon attended the Christian Brothers secondary school in Charleville, and three years later, having won a scholarship, he was supported to enrol in the private school of Blackrock College, where he was to become acquainted with John Charles McQuaid.[8]

John Cooney, in his book *John Charles McQuaid*, writes that McQuaid was born on 28 July 1895 in Cootehill, County Cavan to Dr Eugene McQuaid and his wife Jennie Corry, who died eight days later at the age of twenty-two. In September 1896, fourteen months later, Eugene married Agnes Mayne of Terenure, County Dublin. As she came with a generous dowry, he was able to purchase the parochial house in 1897, following the death of 'Fr Brady, a Maynooth-educated priest who had written pious pamphlets about Faith and Fatherland under the *nom de plume* of Missionary Priest'.[9]

Cooney's research provides insights into the life and times of a typical middle-class family at the turn of the century. McQuaid's father's position of being an educated professional who had access to the intimacies of people's lives, their struggles and their poor health provided a secure base from which John Charles gained knowledge of rural life in Ireland and the social issues that created strain in families and communities. However, within this security, John Charles faced his own challenges.

'As was the case with boys at that time, John was often beaten harshly by his father',[10] who along with being a medical doctor served as a Justice of the Peace and 'built up a reputation as a severe man, not unknown to demand that offenders promise to give up drink, which he considered a root cause of their social degradation'.[11]

In 1905 John Charles finished primary school with a report that read,

His ability to assimilate knowledge was a revelation. With such intellectual attainments this boy will have a brilliant scholastic career and will rise to great heights in whatever profession he adopts.[12]

His second-level education commenced when he departed for St Patrick's boarding school in Cavan a few weeks after his tenth birthday. Before completing his final year there, 'Something untoward happened to John at St Patrick's', and he was taken home by his parents under a cloud of mystery. 'He had suffered a serious breakdown in his physical and emotional outlook.' Looking back on those schooldays shortly before his death, John Charles confided to the writer Mary Purcell:

'If I were to record the barbarities practised in most boys' boarding schools at that time, I might fly this country.' His comments suggest he witnessed – and experienced – physical or sexual abuse.[13]

In October 1910, following months of recuperation in the family home, John Charles, now fifteen, was enrolled in Blackrock College, County Dublin. His parents, Eugene and Agnes, were attracted by an advertisement publicising the college, 'not only for its educational excellence but also for its location overlooking Dublin Bay', where, the prospectus boasted, 'the students can bathe with perfect safety'.[14]

As the summer holidays approached in June 1911, 'the college celebrated its golden jubilee with a Mass at which the Archbishop of Dublin, William Walsh, presided'.[15] During the celebrations that followed, students mixed with prominent former pupils and John Charles probably got his 'first glimpse of the man who would not only shape Ireland's destiny but determine the course of his own career'.[16] That man was Éamon de Valera.

John Charles's time in Blackrock College was brief, and he was to continue his education in Clongowes Wood College, 'where he was accompanied by his half-brother, Dean'.[17] His parents had hoped that the 'switch to Clongowes would broaden his outlook'. They were concerned that he had grown too attached to the elderly Holy Ghost Brother Gaspard, 'known for his devotional extremism'.[18] Brother Gaspard had told John Charles, 'You will have great power in the confessional because of your purity'.[19]

> Downhearted, John was less than fully enthusiastic about his studies at his new school. . . . He missed Brother Gaspard badly.[20]

At the age of sixteen John's academic performance was not what could have been expected.

Further upheaval was to follow:

> In the summer of 1912, the year which saw the sinking of the *Titanic*, John's inner emotional world capsized. He found out that Agnes was not his real mother.[21]

John Charles is reported to have said to a friend at school at the time of receiving this information that:

> My father married a second time. That is bad news for me.[22]

From his research, Cooney observed that this 'revelation had a devastating effect on the introverted teenager', and that he distanced himself from contact with his family. What emerged from this period was 'a moodiness that marked his character in adult life' and 'reinforced his belief that pain and suffering were central to life as God willed it'.[23]

The following year, John Charles established the belief 'that he was called by God to be a missionary priest' and in keeping with a 'pledge to Brother Gaspard to "plant the faith of Christ in the African bush" he 'insisted on joining the Holy Ghost Fathers'.[24] He was ordained a priest in 1924 and a year later was appointed Dean of Studies at Blackrock College. In 1940, he was to become a powerful influence on the political, social and cultural life in Ireland when he was appointed Archbishop of Dublin by Pope Pius XII.

Until his death in 1973, the impact of his influence on the day-to-day life of women and children in the early decades of the Irish Free State cannot be underestimated.

> Dr Noël Browne [Minister for Health from 1948–51] claimed that the most important development in political life during his episcopacy was the relationship established

between himself and de Valera under the 1937 Constitution, when each of them worked together: 'The Church used the State; the State used the Church.'[25]

As 'every childhood lasts a lifetime', the individual experiences Pádraig, Éamon and John Charles had of 'being mothered' is likely to have influenced their thinking on the role of women in family and society. Their personal experiences of being mothered, although varied, reflect those of many families in Victorian Ireland. Common experiences within many families included:

- maternal death arising from childbirth
- silence regarding painful events in the lives of adults
- secrecy surrounding children and details relating to their birth and identity
- abandonment by parents
- emigration of attachment figures
- questions of legitimacy
- all-male boarding schools and seminaries
- physical and sexual abuse being part of life, and being known about and tolerated by wider society
- the priority to educate males
- the expectation that women were to marry, remain in the home and produce children to build a Catholic Nation.

All of these formed the context for the development of Pearse, de Valera and McQuaid and – in the chaotic transition to independent statehood – were valued in daily life. When chaos abounds, the stability of the home comes into focus and provides a secure base from which to act in the wider world. In the Irish Free State, women, mothers and home provided the secure base from which men could force change and/or restrict progress.

At the time when Pádraig Pearse and Éamon de Valera were active in the 1916 Rising, McQuaid had joined the Holy Ghost order at Kimmage Manor, which 'stood in majestic isolation from the capital's populace in accordance with the prevailing orthodoxy that priests were a caste superior to ordinary mortals'.[26]

Cooney writes:

> Like the majority of Irish people, the Holy Ghost Fathers
> were surprised by the armed rising for national indepen-
> dence from Britain, which took place in Dublin in Easter
> Week 1916. The Order's Provincial condemned the Rising
> as the work of 'foolish and uptight men', and one Holy
> Ghost priest denounced it as 'a stab in the back'.

> [However, the] brutal execution of the 1916 leaders swung
> public opinion in favour of the rebels, especially when
> publications such as the Sinn Féin *Catholic Bulletin* pub-
> lished obituaries highlighting the piety they had shown
> before their deaths.[27]

> From autumn 1918 to 1920, turbulent years which saw the
> electoral triumph of Sinn Féin and the outbreak of the War
> of Independence against Britain, McQuaid taught as a pre-
> fect in Blackrock College.[28]

As violence spread across the country, the Holy Ghost schools

> . . . were raided for arms and 'collaborators'. . . The bishops
> meeting at Maynooth, roundly condemned a grim cata-
> logue of British atrocities and declared that the only paral-
> lel to the misdeeds of their 'Black and Tan' troops were the
> outrages of the Bolshevik Red Army.[29]

In the upheaval that followed, the

> . . . Irish Free State became an independent dominion within
> the British Empire . . . though it was still required to profess
> ultimate allegiance to the British Crown, and when the Pres-
> ident of the Executive Government, Éamon de Valera, and

a minority of Sinn Féin refused to accept the Treaty's ratification, the country moved inexorably towards Civil War.[30]

The Civil War ended with a ceasefire rather than a decisive victory. As Free State forces steadily overcame the Anti-Treaty IRA, fighting became a series of skirmishes; IRA leadership, knowing it could not win, ordered its forces to stand down on 30 April 1923. The Civil War lasted for ten months, and claimed the lives of some of the most prominent leaders of the independence movement.[31]

The road to the revolution was energised by the seismic event of the Famine and a steady resistance to rent payments, exportation of agricultural produce and a shifting of Irish identity from being one of oppressed and colonised to being Irish, Gaelic and Catholic.

'The Report of the Commission of Investigation into Mother and Baby Homes' (CIMBH) documents the historical context of that period:

> During the nineteenth century the Catholic church sought to overcome the discrimination that it had experienced under the penal laws. As part of the process it created an infrastructure of Catholic hospitals, orphanages, and other charitable institutions that were designed to ensure that Catholics no longer had to rely on Protestant charities. The British administration in Ireland was willing to delegate the running of institutions, such as industrial schools and nursing services in the workhouses, to female and male Catholic religious communities.[32]

The report further states:

> The nineteenth century was a deeply religious age, marked by increased church attendance, a 'devotional revolution' among Irish Catholics, and a militant evangelical movement among Irish Protestants – which has been described as 'the second reformation'. Catholic and Protestant churches shared a common fear that people in need, especially unmarried mothers and their children, or impoverished widows and destitute married couples, would consent to their children being raised in a different religious denomination in return for economic assistance.[33]

> Religion played a central role in the lives of Irish people. Attendance at Sunday mass and other religious duties was almost universal and many Catholics participated in additional religious observances, such as religious retreats, sodalities, or daily mass during the penitential season of lent. There appears to have been little difference in religious devotion between rich and poor, young and old,

male and female, rural and urban, and this gave the Irish Catholic church an unrivalled position of authority. The authority of the Catholic church undoubtedly increased after 1922. In 1911 Catholics constituted 74 per cent of the population of Ireland; in 1926 they constituted 93 per cent of the population of the Irish Free State.[34]

One factor that secured the high status and wide accep-tance of the Irish Catholic church was the degree to which it reflected the society from which it came and the church's support for key causes – such as national independence, or the importance of prudent marriages that protected a family's property and good standing.[35]

In the decades between the end of the great famine and Irish independence the overall population almost halved; the number of Catholic clergy doubled and the number of religious sisters quadrupled… Many Irish families had a close relative who was a priest, religious sister or a re-ligious brother. In rural parishes the priest was often the best educated member of the community (and the best educated member of his family); in provincial towns he belonged to the tiny educated and social elite.[36]

Many families, faced with a pregnant unmarried daughter, sought their advice, and files reviewed by the Commission of Investigation into Mother and Baby Homes also indicate that 'some women confided in a priest rather than her family'.[37]

The CIMBH reviewed research by K. H. Connell, who argued:

The Irish clergy, who were commonly the sons of mod-estly-comfortable Irish families – middling/strong farmers [and] small-town business men, reflected and reinforced the values of those families in their sermons and general attitudes. The Catholic church and indeed most churches

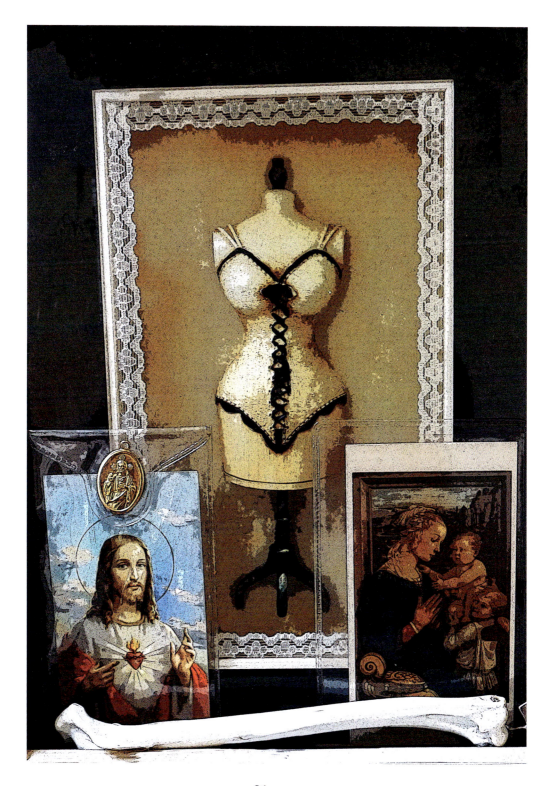

at this time condemned sexual relations outside marriage but in Ireland, Catholic church teaching may have been given additional weight by the social patterns of late marriage, and matchmaking which put a high premium on preventing pre-marital pregnancies, or inappropriate contact between young people.[38]

The Catholic church did not invent Irish attitudes to prudent marriages or family respectability; however, it reinforced them through church teachings that emphasised the importance of pre-marital purity and the sexual dangers associated with dance halls, immodest dress, mixed bathing and other sources of 'temptation'… Priests who denounced a man or woman who was responsible for an extra-marital pregnancy were reinforcing wider social concerns with family lineage and the respectability of a community.[39]

In the 1920s the Irish Free State was a newly independent nation which was determined to show the world that it was different; part of that difference related to the capacity to withstand the undesirable aspects of modernity, including sexual licence and alien cultures. There was a strong alignment of views between church and State, resulting in legislation against contraception, divorce, censorship of cinema and publications that was bolstered by church sermons denouncing sexual immorality and the evils of modern society.[40]

In advance of the 1932 Eucharistic Congress in Dublin, the *Irish Independent* produced a souvenir poster-sized publication to honour the history of the Catholic faith in Ireland and centuries of resistance to British rule. Within the pages of this ninety-year-old document are reports on the celebrations of the centenary of Catholic Emancipation on 23 June 1929. An unnamed reporter wrote that:

. . . the purpose of this great celebration is not merely to commemorate the achievement of 1829, but to recall with gratitude to Almighty God the splendid harvest of Catholic progress whereof the Act of Emancipation was but the sowing.[41]

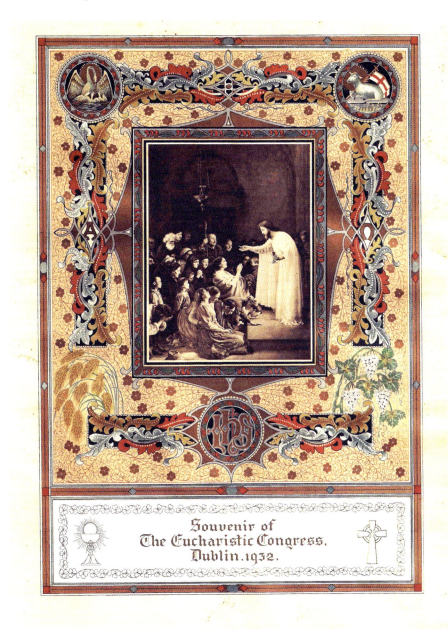

To participate in the celebrations of the centenary of Catholic Emancipation,

> . . . into Dublin poured thousands upon thousands of people by rail and road. Over 50,000 passengers arrived at various railway termini in the city. Many people had been travelling throughout the night, to arrive in the city at such early hours of the morning as 4 o'clock and 5 o'clock. At eight o'clock with a four hours' wait in front of them before the Mass began, many hundreds of people arrived at the Park, and from then until 12 o'clock the human tide moved into the Park. About 1,500 guards and 8,500 stewards controlled the traffic. The Irish Hierarchy led by Most Rev. Dr. MacRory, was in full attendance; the State was represented by Ministers and members of the Oireachtas; practically all

the members of the Diplomatic Corps in Dublin were present; the Judiciary, the Army, the high ranks of the Garda and the professions were all fully represented.[42]

In the course of an inspiring address, Most Rev. Dr Harty said that in celebrating the centenary of Catholic Emancipation they did so in no controversial spirit. They assembled to remember a big event in the history of religious liberty. . . They took the Act as a landmark of the progress of religious liberty and as a symbol of victory over the forces of oppression and bigotry. . . Great enthusiasm prevailed during the demonstration, and the members of the Hierarchy were loudly cheered as they entered the hall and again as they left.[43]

Included in this document are photographs and advertisements, and a number of aspects of the publication stand out. One is the enormous crowd attending the Mass in the Phoenix Park, where a raised altar with tall pillars and domed roof was adorned with a cross and must have been visible for miles. The other is the sense that the content was written entirely by members of the Hierarchy or at least approved by them. Independent journalism is nowhere evident in this national publication and

CONVENT of OUR LADY of CHARITY of REFUGE

ST. MARY'S ASYLUM

High Park

DRUMCONDRA

DUBLIN

At present there are 218 poor penitents in the Asylum absolutely dependent on the Sisters for everything. The Holy Sacrifice of the Mass and the daily prayers of the community and the poor penitents are offered for benefactors living and dead. Donations for the maintenance of this most deserving charity will be thankfully received by the Mother Superior at the Convent. There is a public Laundry attached.

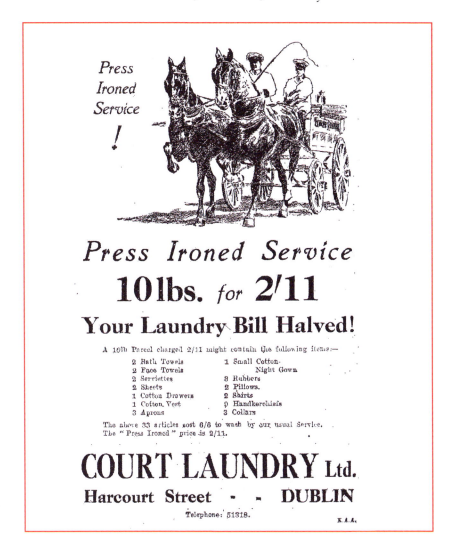

there is little evidence of women and no words reported as having been uttered by a woman. Women are referenced in some diverse advertising, such as household drapery, hair tonic for 'lustrous radiance', and new sable furs for sale at a well-known Dublin boutique.

At the other end of the spectrum are advertisements for Magdalen Laundries. One invites charitable donations to those who provided shelter to the 'Penitents' who lived within St Mary's Asylum. The 'Pentitents' included unmarried mothers, homeless and destitute women and girls and older women who had no-where else to call home.

These two advertisements give testament to the existence of Magdalen Laundries prior to the emergence of the Irish Free State.

The fundamental conflicts in human life are not between competing ideas – one of which is true and the other false, but rather, between those that hold power and use it to oppress others, and those who are oppressed by power and seek to free themselves of it.

– Phyllis Chesler [44]

One of the least-spoken-about oppressions of women's soul lives concerns millions of unmarried or never-married mothers throughout the world … who … in this century alone, were pressured by cultural mores to hide their condition or their children, or else kill or surrender their offspring, or to live a half-life under assumed identities and as reviled and disempowered citizens.

– Clarissa Pinkola Estés[45]

2.

THERE WAS A YOUNG WOMAN

There was a young woman who lived in the woods
A weelya, weelya, wallya
There was a young woman who lived in the woods
Down by the River Saulya

She had a baby three months old
A weelya, weelya, wallya
She had a baby three months old
Down by the River Saulya

She stuck a knife in the baby's heart
A weelya, weelya, wallya
She stuck a knife in the baby's heart
Down by the River Saulya

Three big policemen knockin' on the door
A weelya, weelya, wallya
Three big policemen knockin' on the door
Down by the River Saulya

Are you the woman that killed the child?
A weelya, weelya, wallya
Are you the woman that killed the child?
Down by the River Saulya

Yes I'm the woman that killed the child
A weelya, weelya, wallya
Yes I'm the woman that killed the child
Down by the River Saulya

They put a rope around her neck
A weelya, weelya, wallya
They put a rope around her neck
Down by the River Saulya

They pulled the rope and she got hung
A weelya, weelya, wallya
They pulled the rope and she got hung
Down by the River Saulya

And that was the end of the woman in the woods
A weelya, weelya, wallya
And that was the end of the woman in the woods
Down by the River Saulya

Versions of this song have circulated in a variety of ways. The one above has been adapted and spelling changed to aid reading and rhythm.

There are songs that fade from schoolyard memories, songs that we sang as children in the 1960s and 1970s which reflected a culture we took for granted. These words, chanted aloud, supported our rhythm as we jumped the skipping-rope, 'There was a young woman, who lived in the woods, a weelya, weelya, wallya...'

To us as children, these were just words of a playground ditty which contained a sense of menace, like a fairy tale with a wicked witch. However, as culture is passed on through story and song, the words reveal a reality known to many across Ireland in the decades that followed the establishment of the Free State in 1922. This reality was infanticide.

Alexis Guilbride, in her chapter 'Infanticide: The Crime of Motherhood' in *Motherhood in Ireland*, writes:

> While infanticide was a woman's crime, the criminal justice system of the new state was controlled and operated exclusively by men. What is most striking in the legal records of infanticide cases of the period, however, is the absence of the male. The courts did not consider the question of who fathered the infants whose deaths were being investigated relevant. Fathers and brothers of the accused were invariably assumed to be ignorant of the matter, while mothers and sisters often colluded with the birth mother in the concealment of the birth and the disposal of the body. In a number of cases, it was the mother of the woman who had just given birth who was charged with the murder of the infant.[1]

Guilbride reflects on the context for this practice and observes that the connection between Church and State was

> . . . based on a nationalist, cultural tradition located in the myth of a golden, rural past. Within this tradition, to be Gaelic was to be Catholic, and to be a woman was to be subject to the dictates of a philosophy that sanctified the primacy of the male and the subjection of the female... Sexual morality, or the control of women's bodies, thus became one of the central political issues of the ensuing decades in the new Ireland, and it remains so up the present day.[2]

As the Irish Free State settled into existence, the collaboration between Church and State began to tighten its grip on human rights and particularly women's rights:

> The first of a series of repressive acts passed by the state in post-independence Ireland was the Censorship of Films Act 1923. This act paved the way for the infamous Censorship of Publications Act of 1929, which made the publishing, sale and distribution of literature advocating birth control a criminal offence.[3]

In Ireland, an island nation isolated from the world, infanticide as a means of family planning, and protecting a family's 'good name' and a girl's prospect of marriage, was to remain a feature of urban and rural life for decades.

Guilbride continues:

> In 1935, Section 17 of the Criminal Law Amendments Act finally outlawed the importation, the sale and distribution of contraceptive devices of any sort. The blatant misogyny enshrined in these statutes was not lost on the few remaining representatives of a more enlightened Irish cultural tradition than that which held sway in the post-independence era.[4]

Referencing the work of John Lyons, Guilbride writes that,

> . . . during a debate in the senate in 1928 on the Censorship of Publications Bill, Gogarty was moved to comment: 'I think it is high time that the people of this country find some other way of loving God than by hating women.'[5]

Following Irish independence, work was also underway on making amendments to the Children Act of 1908 to give some powers to local government and public health. 'The Report of the Commission of Investigation into Mother and Baby Homes' states:

> During the second reading in the Seanad, Sir E. Coey Bigger, former chief medical officer of the Irish Local Government Board, expressed the opinion that the Bill 'may reduce very materially the death rate of illegitimate children. These children are not wanted, they are boarded out, and if they died so much the better'. He described the Bill as a 'good one'.[6]

The Illegitimate Children's (Affiliation Orders) Bill came before the Seanad in 1929. In theory it would recognise that women could seek support from the father of their child.

> In practice, however, an affiliation order (one which recognised the father's relationship with the child) proved virtually impossible to pursue and, accordingly, failed to provide women in this situation with any redress, or indeed, any means of survival.[7]

Senator Gogarty saw the enactment of this Bill 'as one which would reduce the cases of infanticide around the country'. According to J. B. Lyons, he told the senate:

> There is an appalling condition of affairs in this country, and that is infanticide. Anything that will give the mother a chance and will encourage her to preserve the life of the child and not strangle it deserves our consideration.[8]

As reported incidents of infanticide continued to rise, Guilbride, referencing the works of others, writes:

> One judge, whose comments on the subject were reported in the *Cork Examiner* in 1929, claimed that: 'The number of newly-born infants in the country who were murdered by their mother at present surpassed belief. Only one out of fifty came up in the courts, but there was a wholesale slaughter of these innocents going on through the country'.[9]

Fear of an illegitimate pregnancy becoming exposed in the local community is a theme that runs through court reports of the early decades of the Irish Free State. Ferriter writes that 'it is clear the fear of being branded the parent of an illegitimate child drove young women to desperation.'[10] The CIMBH report observed that women pregnant outside of marriage were thrown a life-line by The Legitimacy Act 1931, which

> . . . provided that the child of a single mother was 'legitimate' if the parents married within ten months of the birth.[11]

This of course required the willingness and consent of the father of the child. Such weddings were often referred to as 'shotgun' weddings. In *Occasions of Sin*, Ferriter writes:

> From 1920 to 1930, the average number of illegitimate births per annum in the twenty-six counties was deemed to be 1,706. But this rose to 1,853 between 1926 and 1929. These figures do not take into consideration 'shotgun weddings', pregnancy emigration, abortion and infanticide.[12]

Those in government in the Irish Free State formed the view that the solution to the problem of illegitimate births rested with

> . . . the establishment of antenatal homes for expectant un-married mothers and institutions where the mother and children 'might be maintained together for at least the first year of the child's life' (the idea being that the child could then be fostered).[13]

The report of CIMBH states:

> The significance of the coincidence between the establish-ment of mother and baby homes and Irish independence should not be overstated. Mother and baby homes were not an Irish solution to an Irish problem; Ireland was late in establishing mother and baby homes and the initial rec-ommendation in favour of these special homes came from the 1906 Vice-Regal Commission on the Irish Poor Law.[14]

As the provision of a service for unmarried mothers evolved, the state's acceptance of proposals to establish ante-natal homes

> . . . laid the foundation for the infrastructure of religious order-run mother and baby homes that operated from 1922 until the 1970s. . . The priority was to avoid mix-ing 'redeemable' and 'unreformable' sinners (those who had more than one illegitimate pregnancy), with the 'un-reformable' being sent to the Magdalens (along with the 'mentally deficient').[15]

The report of the CIMBH documents that:

In 1933, Bishop Fogarty of Killaloe divided unmarried mothers into three categories: a large number who were a 'feeble or weak-willed sort . . . never be able to take care of themselves . . . easy victims of the wicked'. He believed that they should be placed in institutions under the care of religious sisters though he claimed that no such institutions existed. A second category were 'naturally decent . . . who have fallen through accident or environment'. Sean Ross [mother and baby home] would deal with these 'girls'. The third class were 'women of a wild and vicious nature, who are a harmful influence wherever they prevail. They are neither amenable to religion outside, nor will they consent to abide permanently in religious institutions'; he noted some of these women were admitted to homes run by the Good Shepherd Nuns (Magdalen Homes).[16]

When a mother is forced to choose between the child and the culture, there is something abhorrently cruel and unconsidered about that culture. A culture that requires harm to one's soul in order to follow the culture's proscriptions is a very sick culture indeed. This 'culture' can be the one the woman lives in, but more damning yet, it can be the one she carries around and complies with within her own mind.

Clarissa Pinkola Estés[17]

3.

WOMEN AND CHILDREN FIRST

Emigration has been a feature of Irish life for generations. In the years following the establishment of the Irish Free State in 1922, the drainage of youth from urban and rural areas continued, only now, it was under Irish administration. This required a rethink by the authorities on the reasons behind the vast numbers that continued to leave these shores.

Pauline Conroy, in her chapter 'Maternity Confined: The Struggle for Fertility Control' in *Motherhood in Ireland*, presents some stark statistics:

> Between 1926 and 1936, 57 per cent of emigrants were women and girls, the majority aged 16 to 24 years.[1]

And according to Alexis Guilbride in the same volume:

> Throughout the 1920s and 1930s pregnant Irish women made the journey to Britain in considerable numbers, either to have abortions which, although illegal, were still more widely available there than in Ireland, or to have their babies and give them up for adoption.[2]

The haemorrhaging of young people, and especially young women, was debated and considered by government and Church hierarchy. The consequences of depopulation on social

and economic life in rural and urban areas was acutely felt. In addition to these outcomes were concerns regarding the reputation of the newly emerging nation, but the cold, hard statistics contained difficult truths. In *Occasions of Sin*, Diarmaid Ferrier states:

> Reports sent to Archbishop Byrne in the 1920s concerning the work of the Port and Station Worker Society reveal that, between 1922 and 1927, of the 3,420 women the society helped at the English ports, 2,292 were Irish.[3]

In 1956, the Garda Commissioner, in a letter to the Taoiseach, divided

> . . . Irish emigrants into just two categories: those whose forebears were 'driven to the mountains and bogs by Cromwell and have been living on uneconomic holdings', and those 'who did not accept Irish institutions and laws, and preferred to live elsewhere'.[4]

Ireland's reputation in England came under scrutiny as wave after wave of unmarried pregnant girls required charitable and local government supports. The Commission of Investigation into Mother and Baby Homes (CIMBH) examined a series of articles written by Gertrude Gaffney in 1936. These articles referred to the experience of Irish women 'pregnant-on-arrival' in England.

> One article which concentrated on pregnant single women, and was titled, 'Unchristian attitude of parents': 'All priests, nuns, and lay people connected with the rescue work in London spoke with great severity of the unchristian and inhuman attitude in Ireland towards the unmarried mother, and declared that this attitude made their problem so much more difficult and gave the girl or child

very little chance of making good. . . . The Englishman takes his responsibility in these matters. The Irishman gets off scot free; he has the same callousness as the parents and the relatives, and everything is done to encourage that callousness.'[5]

According to Alexis Guilbride, the war years (1939–1945) presented particular challenges for unmarried pregnant women and girls in Ireland. With the twenty-six-county State asserting its neutrality,

> . . . the Emergency Powers Act came into effect in Ireland and severe restrictions were placed on travel to Britain. Consequently, the illegitimacy rate in Ireland increased significantly during the war years, as did the trade in back street abortions. But the most dramatic increase in this area was evidenced by the numbers of women appearing before the courts on charges of infanticide. From 1940 to 1946, the years of the travel ban, legal records indicate at least forty-six cases of infanticide coming before the Central Criminal Court, whereas fewer than twenty such cases were tried during the previous fifteen years.[6]

The CIMBH report states:

> Between 1939 and 1942 the number of 'illegitimate' births registered increased from 1,761 (0.61 per 1,000) to 2,419 (0.82 per 1,000) and continued to rise, peaking in 1946 to 2,642 (0.9 per 1,000).[7]

When the restrictions of the Emergency Powers Act eased, the ports saw the flood of emigrants resume. Pauline Conroy states:

> In the period 1946 to 1951, women made up 58 per cent of all emigrants. During the period between 1926 and 1961,

some 0.4 million women and girls left Ireland. The representation of women among emigrants from Ireland is one of the few social, economic or political spaces where women achieved parity with men.[8]

Ferriter writes that back in Dublin there was

. . . consternation about the plight of the vulnerable and 'fallen' Irish. A particular concern was with what were believed to be 'seductive advertisements' for girls to work abroad – one of the issues raised by popular Irish journalist Aodh de Blacam when contributing to a government sub-committee on rural depopulation in 1947. The following year a proposal to ban emigration of women under the age of 21 (who accounted for 35 per cent of those leaving) was considered on 'moral, social and demographic grounds'; an idea prompted by figures that showed that the out-flow of female workers had increased from 10,609 in 1945 to 19,205 in 1946 with a slight drop to 18,727 in 1947, about 70 per cent of whom were domestic servants.[9]

Archbishop John Charles McQuaid regarded reports of the conditions of Irish emigrants to England as 'nuisance value', and

> . . . later noted that by 1954 the [Emigrant Welfare] bureau had looked after about 110,000 people. But the English charities had their own concerns about the Irish girls, especially those who arrived pregnant. Over a 25-day period in October 1948, for example, 48 pregnant Irish women had applied to the English Catholic charity, the Crusade of Rescue, many of them described as 'of the cheeky type', while at the Sacred Heart convent in west Hull, 85 of the 89 children baptised between March and September 1948 were born to Irish girls who were pregnant when they arrived.[10]

The 'cheeky type' suggests resilience and persistence to overcome adversity. The alternative labelling which was commonly used to describe unmarried mothers in Ireland at the time were

. . . 'unfortunate creatures, unhappy sisters, fallen women, defiled wreck', all convey a picture of victims who were in this position due to their ignorance and trustfulness, often having been betrayed by wicked men. They were portrayed as pathetic, aimless women, who wandered the streets like 'withered leaves driven in the wind', or drifted about like 'derelict vessels'. They had lost their sexual purity, and with it their sense of direction and purpose.[11]

The report of the CIMBH states:

> Many pregnant women fled to Britain, to protect their se-
> crecy, only to face the prospect of being returned to Ireland
> against their wishes. There is no other known instance
> where substantial numbers of pregnant women fled their
> country, though it was common elsewhere for women to
> move from their home place, generally to a city, in search
> of anonymity. British Catholic charities put considerable
> pressure on Irish Hierarchy and on the government to re-
> patriate the women.[12]

Ferriter presents numbers that reflect the reality of pregnant
emigrants and the depth of concern for their safety and welfare:

> In 1952 the Catholic Rescue and Protection Society had re-
> patriated 85 mothers and their babies but 'there were many
> times that number who refused to return to Ireland . . . se-
> crecy is the unmarried mother's first and greatest need'.[13]

> During 1953, the Liverpool Vigilance Association, which
> forwarded to the [Emigrant Welfare] bureau the names
> and addresses of the Irish girls it encountered, sent 530
> such names, mostly girls aged 16 or 17 who arrived with
> nothing but a 'few shillings in their pockets'.[14]

> The bureau was prepared to pay the fares home of girls 'if
> moral danger was established'. There was also an aware-
> ness that many a married woman was anxious to travel to
> English cities to join her husband due to 'anxiety in regard
> to her husband's conduct'.[15]

> Of the 3,291 women who applied to the Westminster Cru-
> sade of Rescue between 1950 and 1953, more than half
> (1,693) were Irish. Cardinal Griffin, the Archbishop of

Westminster, suggested that such girls had 'too great a fear' of the Irish clergy, and that 'too narrow a view' was taken of their 'offence' in Ireland.[16]

The risks these girls and young women faced is clearly illustrated in the following research recorded by Ferriter:

A three part series in the *Manchester Guardian* in April 1955 reported on 'destitute Irish girls ("these deplorable unsponsored arrivals")' who went 'on the streets within a week or so of their arrival'. Eight years later, it was suggested that one-sixth of the prostitutes coming before the courts in London were Irish.[17]

The parish priest of Camden referred to 'an organised effort' made at Euston Station to 'capture' young Irish girls for prostitution.[18]

Back in Irish ports, the persistent practice of boat-loads of young women and girls departing, pregnant, unwed and often abandoned by boyfriends and families, continued unabated. The integration of government and Church authority allowed little room for consideration of human rights and equality, which in turn replicated a cultural bias of valuing the male over the female and land ownership over loyalty to family members. This bias continued to allow for exposure of girls, women and their infants and 'illegitimate' children, to extreme risk and abandonment by kin.

A major event in Ireland during the Emergency Years was the appointment of John Charles McQuaid as Archbishop of Dublin by Pope Pius XII. In 1940, John Charles 'chose December 27, the feast of John the Evangelist, as the day of his consecration'.[19] He was to assert his authority over political processes and health and education services for decades, until obliged to step down by the Vatican in 1972. In the intervening years, Ferriter writes,

> . . . those seeking to ask questions about the welfare of the vulnerable inevitably found themselves stepping on the toes of the powerful Archbishop McQuaid. . . . Those who were intent on raising difficult issues like the welfare of young women were dismissed by McQuaid and his colleagues as interfering busybodies who had too much time on their hands and were not of the True Faith.[20]

McQuaid's archives include information on the fortunes of emigrants as reported by Hubert Daly of the Legion of Mary:

> Daly was frank about the prevailing view among priests and nuns in England that Irish girls seemed to have little sense of commitment to their religion or country; 'one could sense an undertone of contempt for the whole set-up in Ireland which is producing so many young people who fail to live up to the ideals which they are supposed to be taught in Ireland'.[21]

These words reflect a significant 'blind spot' in the thinking of the Church hierarchy and those in leadership in Ireland. They place shame and blame entirely on the shoulders of the unmarried and pregnant girls and women who were rejected and abandoned by families, lovers, friends and community. They fail to appreciate that some of the young women were victims of sexual crime and many did not have any information about

the possible consequences of sexual intercourse, pregnancy or childbirth. They also suggest a total disregard to the reality that another person – the child – required care, consideration and protection.

The CIMBH reports that:

> In 1969 Fr Eoin Sweeney, who had worked for some years as a chaplain to Irish emigrants in England, published a short paper in the Catholic journal *The Furrow* on 'The pastoral care of unmarried mothers': 'The unmarried mother is not a prodigy. She has always been a factor in society, in every social category, and always will be. Education, profession or social stature is not a guarantee against this misfortune. And the average girl to whom this happens is a perfectly normal girl, not a psychiatric case. However, from the moment that she first realises her plight, she goes through a period of intense strain, sometimes verging on desperation.'[22]

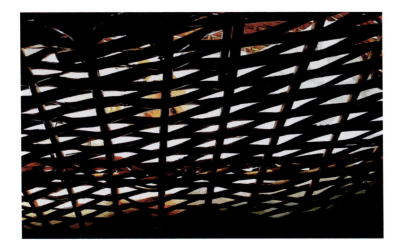

By the late 1960s there is emerging evidence of a more sympathetic attitude towards unmarried mothers on the part of some Catholic clergy. This change in attitude reflects greater activism among some Catholic priests about social issues, such as housing, poverty and rural decline, plus the fact that a growing number of priests had worked as pastors to Irish emigrants in Britain, where they were confronted with a variety of personal and social problems, including unmarried mothers. The introduction of liberal access to abortion in Britain in 1967, and evidence that unmarried pregnant Irish women were seeking abortions in Britain, was also a factor prompting greater sympathy towards unmarried women who continued with their pregnancy.[23]

However, change was to proceed at a much slower pace in Ireland, with attitudes of rejection and exile to persist for at least another decade.

In 1971 Fr Barrett [Director of the Catholic Social Welfare Bureau] claimed that 'Parents are not overly sympathetic to pregnant daughters and those allowing them to come home are very small'.[24]

Women have died a thousand deaths before they are twenty years old. They've gone in this direction or that, and have been cut off. They have hopes and dreams that have been cut off also. Anyone who says otherwise is still asleep... While all these things deepen individuation, differentiation, growing up and growing out, blossoming, becoming awake and aware and conscious, they are also profound tragedies and have to be grieved as such.

– Clarissa Pinkola Estés[25]

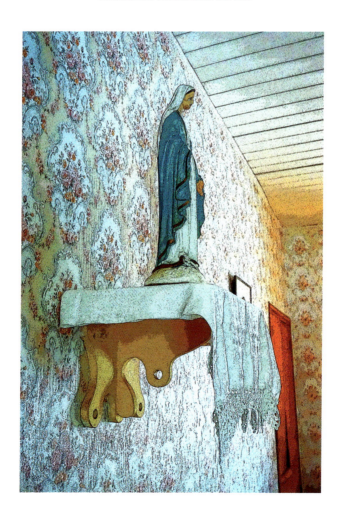

4.

FROM CRISIS TO CONSTITUTION TO CATHOLIC CONTROLS

When Pádraig Pearse and those defiant brothers-in-arms occupied the General Post Office during the Easter Rising in 1916, their aspirations were documented within the proclamation of 'The Provisional Government of the Irish Republic, to the People of Ireland'. Their words captured the hopes and dreams of generations of Irish men and women. Within the declaration they presented a Republic which

> . . . guarantees religious and civil liberty, equal rights and equal opportunities to all its citizens, and declares its resolve to pursue the happiness and prosperity of the whole nation and of all its parts, cherishing all the children of the nation equally, and oblivious of the differences carefully fostered by an alien government, which have divided the minority from the majority in the past.[1]

These are noble words that might lay the foundation for a constitution which reflects human rights and equal opportunities and an absence of discrimination against 'illegitimate' infants and their unmarried mothers.

However, John Cooney explains that a year after the establishment of the Irish Free State in 1922, attempts

. . . by the Attorney General, Hugh Kennedy, to preserve for Protestants a parliamentary procedure granting marriage dissolutions with a right to remarry were scuppered by the Hierarchy.[2]

Referring to the research of Keogh, Alexis Guilbride writes that:

. . . the ruling party in the new state, had sought the advice of the hierarchy on the issue of divorce and in October 1923, their lordships, the bishops issued a statement which proclaimed: 'The Bishops of Ireland have to say that it would be altogether unworthy of an Irish legislative body to sanction the concession of such divorce, no matter who the petitioners may be.'[3]

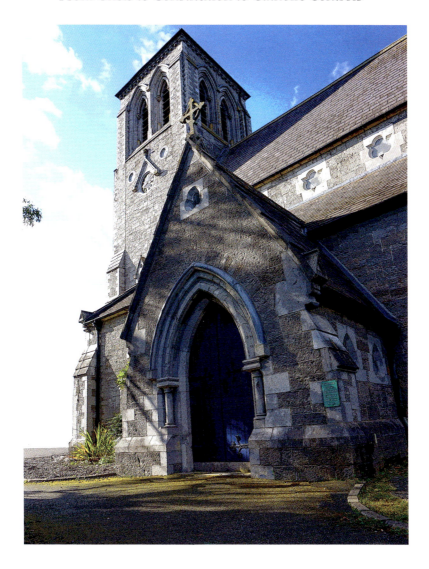

By 1925, a motion was carried in the Dáil preventing the introduction of private divorce bills to the Irish parliament. So, from the very beginning, the government of a newly independent Ireland was entering into consultation with the hierarchy to seek the advice and approval of the Catholic Church with regard to how an 'Irish legislative body' (as distinct from a British legislative body) should order its affairs.[4]

Cooney adds that Free State

> . . . politicians were receptive to the claims of the Catholic Church in society. Already underway was a process of State abdication of its authority. In the immediate post-independence period Cosgrave [President of the Executive Council] had considered giving the Vatican the power of veto over legislation contrary to faith and morals in return for Papal recognition of the new State.[5]

The catholicisation of the Free State proceeded steadily. In 1923 a law on film censorship was approved. In 1924 and 1927 laws curtailing the consumption of strong alcoholic drink were introduced at the prompting of the bishops. By 1926 the census showed that the Protestant population had begun to decline, and over the next decades would fall from 11 per cent of the population to around 5 per cent.[6]

Control of the hearts and minds of the citizens of Ireland, who were burdened with the duty to 'go forth and multiply' (Genesis 1:28) and pass on the faith to generations of unquestioning citizens of an emerging nation, remained a central focus of the Church authorities.

In his research into the character and influence of Archbishop John Charles McQuaid, John Cooney writes that he and other members of the Hierarchy

> . . . looked to de Valera as the political leader who would create the Catholic social order – now being called 'vocationalism', in the Free State. They were encouraged in this expectation by Fianna Fáil's deputy leader, Seán T. O'Kelly, who claimed during the [1932] general election campaign that 'our policy was that of Pope Pius XI'. The perception of an alliance between Catholicism and Fianna Fáil was reinforced when Seán MacEntee boasted that the party had won 'the Catholic vote'.[7]

Cooney observed that:

> Triumphalism was becoming the dominant characteristic
> of Catholicism in the Free State, which was also submit-
> ting its social mores to the control of the clergy and a de-
> vout laity – described by the writers Liam O'Flaherty and
> Peadar O'Donnell, respectively but not respectfully as 'the
> soutaned bullies of the Lord' and the 'yahoo laity'.[8]

Cooney continues:

> By 1934, McQuaid's friendship with de Valera was so close to allow him privately to make numerous attempts to influence the head of Government's attitude to matters of public policy. 'I am grateful for the kindness that allows me to make such suggestions,' McQuaid wrote in November after drawing de Valera's attention to 'discontent' over the Criminal Amendment Bill's proposal that contraceptives could be imported freely once they were not for sale.

McQuaid was

> . . . worried about the provision that the Post Office could not in that event open a package, he proposed that the phrase 'for sale' should be deleted. He wanted the Post Office to have an automatic right of search so that no contraceptives could be sent to private individuals for personal use from Britain or elsewhere.[9]

Pauline Conroy writes:

> Despite advice not to introduce a total ban on contraception, a proposal to outlaw contraception was put before the Dáil, with the following words: It shall not be lawful for any person to sell, or expose, offer, advertise or keep for sale, or to import or attempt to import into Saorstat Éireann for sale, any contraceptive.[10]

> In Ireland, contraception was first banned by Section 17 (1) of the 1935 Criminal Law Amendment Act. The Criminal Law Amendment Bill was introduced by Fianna Fáil in 1934 and was described as a 'Bill . . . for the protection and suppression of brothels and prostitution and for those

and other purposes to amend the law relating to sexual offences' (Saorstat Éireann, 1934)[11]

The work of reform of legislation inherited from the previous administration continued throughout the 1930s and the drafting of the Irish Constitution became a focal point for Church–State collaboration during those years. Cooney writes:

From early 1937, Éamon de Valera was bombarded with letters almost daily – sometimes twice a day – from Fr John McQuaid C.S.Sp. They were crammed with suggestions, viewpoints, documents and learned references on nearly

every aspect of what was to become *Bunreacht na h'Éireann*
– the Constitution of Ireland. McQuaid was the persistent
adviser, 'one of the great architects of the Constitution
albeit in the shadows.' However, McQuaid's efforts to
enshrine the absolute claims of the Catholic Church as the
Church of Christ were frustrated by de Valera.[12]

McQuaid's Catholic and nationalist fingerprints were everywhere in the new *Bunreacht*, third only to those of de
Valera and his chief draughtsman, John Hearne.[13]

In an early draft, McQuaid anchored the concept of family in the traditional model of 'a valid marriage' – a husband, wife and four or five children, the average size in late 1930s Ireland. He proposed that: 'The State guarantees the constitution and protection of the family as the basis of moral education and social discipline and harmony, and the sure foundation of ordered society.'[14]

In her analysis of the legislative framework that impacted on the lives of women, Conroy writes:

> By 1936, a well-fenced package of legislative barriers to the advancement of the status of women in production and reproduction had been put in place. This package was the prelude to the insertion into the 1937 constitution of clauses which prescribed the place of mothers as in the home and omitted any reference to equality between women and men. Far from the 1937 constitution being the onset of the formal exclusion of women from economic, cultural and social life, it was the culmination of a discriminatory process.[15]

This attitude towards women's active participation in wider society, Guilbride writes, 'found explicit expression in Article 41 of the constitution of 1937, which states':

> Article 41.1: In particular, the State recognises that, by her life within the home, woman gives to the State a support without which the common good cannot be achieved.
>
> Article 41.2 : The State shall, therefore, endeavour to ensure that mothers shall not be obliged by economic necessity to engage in labour to the neglect of their duties in the home (Bunreacht na hÉireann, 1937).[16]

Pauline Conroy presented this analysis:

> As a newly founded state, Saorstat Éireann, had to iden-
> tify, plan, form and construct an armoury of bans, ex-
> clusions and prohibitions to the integration of women
> and girls into the economic, social, cultural and political
> life of the state. Control over women's fertility in all its
> aspects was an essential ingredient within this strategy,
> which was complemented by control over jobs, juries,
> property, social security, education and training. This
> socio-legal structure remained relatively intact until
> the late 1960s... At work and at home, laws and regula-
> tions akin to fundamentalism circumscribed the lives of
> women and girls.[17]

The influence of the Church hierarchy on the formulation of legislation is well recorded by others. This influence was also structural as it extended into the daily lives of Catholic pa-rishioners. At a local level, through diocese and parish-based activities, the hierarchy promoted many channels through which its authority could be exercised and monitored. Daily, weekly and monthly practices and rituals formed part of these controls.

This author recalls that while growing up in Ireland in the 1960s and 1970s the nightly drop to the knees by the entire family to recite the Rosary was a central pillar of these con-trols, as was the twice-daily recitation of the Angelus, when the national broadcaster paused to have the sound of bells call the faithful to prayer. To this day, the bells continue to be broadcast at 12 noon and 6.00 pm by Radió Teilifís Éireann (RTÉ).

At Sunday Mass, girls and women were required to wear a triangle of black lace called a 'mantilla' on their head. During the long sermons my little fingers would reach up to trace the lace-edges on both shoulders. There were five mantillas in our home and these were folded up and returned to a brown envelope in the hall table drawer after Mass. Also near the front door was a Holy Water font, into which we dipped an index finger; then, making the sign of the cross on ourselves, we left the house. A string of blue wool was worn around our necks and under our clothes. On this was secured a 'miraculous medal', which depicted an image of the Blessed Virgin Mary. We wore this to 'protect us from all harm'.

Lenten Missions were an annual event attended mostly by adults in packed churches throughout the country. Standing in the raised pulpit among the congregation, the priest would lecture on the evils of the flesh and the wrath of God. There are memories of a shouting priest decrying the potential loss of sperm when young men 'pleasure themselves' (masturbate). What was not articulated but nonetheless conveyed was that this was sperm that would be better deposited into a womb to create another Catholic child for Ireland.

Sacrifice and penance was required by all, even the youngest child, for those weeks coming up to Easter, and all sweet treats were to be denied or at least stored in a location unknown to siblings, for fear of a secret raid by the less disciplined members. The national broadcaster played hours of solemn requiem music in the days directly before Easter Sunday and we observed total silence for an hour on the afternoons of those sunny Good Fridays of childhood memories.

The annual Corpus Christi Procession along the main street following an ornately robed priest, while loudly praying the Rosary and singing hymns, was a requirement for the entire community. Children who had recently 'made their communion' would be the first group in line, dressed in white dresses and smart suits; the girls and boys joined their hands in prayer and focused their eyes on the monstrance held aloft by the priest.

The monstrance was a gold or highly polished, sun-shaped brass object on a base. Inside the centre of the sun shape was a circular pane of glass on a hinged door. Inside this was a piece of

Holy Communion bread, which represented the body of Christ. The priest led the procession along the street, all the while protected under a yellow velvet canopy trimmed with golden tassels. Each of the four corners of the canopy had a brass leg, and each of these was held by a priest-in-training or a suited man.

Shop owners along the street would enter into the spirit of the occasion by decorating their windows with religious pictures and statues and yellow and white flowers, as a nod to the Vatican flag. Also along the street, secured to post and telegraph poles, were loud speakers in the form of upturned rectangular buckets.

These were to ensure that those who lined the footpaths and followed the crowd could partake of the prayers and singing, led by the priest, who was wired for sound.

The burden of responsibility to fulfil and pass on these demands and rituals was placed on the lap of the married mothers of Ireland. It was the married mothers' duty to pass on the faith in order to ensure her children would make it through the gates of Heaven. It was married mothers' duty to honour the father, promote self-discipline and restraint and ensure the forgiveness of sins of her offspring through confession. The requirement to confess sins (sometimes invented) to a partially hidden priest in the confession box was a monthly expectation.

Betty Hilliard, in her chapter 'Motherhood, Sexuality and the Catholic Church' in *Motherhood in Ireland*, writes:

> Foucault (1976) has identified the development of an internalised compulsion to confession in early modern western society as a means of policing sexual activity, among other things… The power of the confessional in this regard, at least up until the 1970s, was evidenced in the fact that the majority of respondents [to a study undertaken by Hillard] felt it incumbent on them to confess their attempts at limiting family size.[18]

In the study, Hilliard explored

> . . . the experiences of a sample of mothers in Cork City, who were interviewed as part of a project on family research in 2000. These women had first become mothers mainly in the 1950s and 1960s, decades before the impact of feminism and the availability of contraceptives in the Republic; the birth rate was high among these women and motherhood was the central role of their lives.[19]

Hilliard's study found that:

> A central issue in these women's lives was their belief that avoidance of pregnancy was viewed by the Catholic Church as sinful: sex was for procreation.[20]

Women interviewed in the study reported that,

> 'You had to go [to confession].'

> This experience was in the main a very unhappy one:

> 'I dreaded going to confession. . . . I did have to say it to them that I was avoiding having children.'

> 'I dreaded going.'

> 'We were scared to go to confession.'

The main reason for this dread was that the stark choice in many cases was either to resolve to stop avoiding further pregnancies or to be refused absolution. For many women in this predicament, they already had large families and found it extremely difficult to provide for them.[21]

Hilliard's research found among the women that:

It was also perceived as a sin to decline sexual activity against the wishes of one's husband: 'Women couldn't say no to their husbands no matter how bad they felt or anything. It was a sin.'[22]

A further indignity imposed on the married mothers of Ireland was the practice of 'churching'. Hilliard describes women who having achieved the desired result of producing another Catholic child for Ireland, then had to endure 'the custom of a woman going to church for a blessing after the birth of a child'. Her research findings indicated

. . . it was perceived in negative terms as a form of purification: You couldn't go outside the door until you were churched. Your mother wouldn't let you. You were made to feel guilty. It was done at the small altar. They'd bless you for having been a bad person (for having the baby).[23]

There were eight children in our family and fourteen were born into our neighbour's tiny house. From the laneways of towns and cities, lined with three-roomed houses, hordes of children spilled onto the streets in different states of attire, hygiene and health. Many of the good Catholic women of Ireland were frequent visitors to the doctor in search of tablets for 'the nerves'. Many more were to see their young adult offspring take the boat across the sea, never to return.

Patriarchy is the power of the fathers: a familial-social, ideological, political system in which men – by force, direct pressure, or through ritual, tradition, law, and language, customs, etiquette, education, and the division of labor, determine what part women shall or shall not play, and in which the female is everywhere subsumed under the male. It does not necessarily imply that no woman has power, or that all women in a given culture may not have certain powers.

Adrienne Rich[24]

Referring to the influence of Sigmund Freud on how mental health professionals have considered women's issues, Phyllis Chesler, responds to a question he raised 'What do women want'? She replies, 'For starters, and in no particular order: freedom, food, nature, shelter, leisure, freedom from violence, justice, music, poetry, supportive families and communities, compassionate support during chronic or life threatening illness and at the time of death, independence, books, physical/sexual pleasure, education, solitude, the ability to defend ourselves, love, ethical friendships, the arts, health, dignified and useful employment, political friendships.

Phyllis Chesler[25]

5.

MORE THAN WORDS

Some say that Ireland, this small green island on the north-west edge of Europe, holds the secret to excellence in literature. Reflecting on the history of Ireland, one wonders how this has come to pass? Some say it has to do with the subterranean emotional space the Irish held watch over during the centuries of British administration. That space where folklore, place names, the ancient Gaelic language and its lyrical description of life events and of place supported the sense of kinship and ownership over land and story. That place where the external world of rent payment, taxes, starvation and emigration told one part of the story, while music, song, dance, folklore, absence of family members and a sensory engagement with the environment was wildly wrapped around the entire experience and has found a form of expression on the pages of Irish writers.

It is perplexing then to think that once the Free State was established, the authorities wasted little time in banning books, many of them written by Irish writers. Did we not want to hear ourselves think? Perhaps those decades of suppression of expression have once again energised the subterranean emotional space the Irish hold dear and have nurtured in quiet and imaginative thoughts for centuries?

Like a dam holding back a torrent, the silenced words and thoughts are now free to find a home on the page. We live in a time when the gagged women and children contained by institutions have shown us how to speak the unspeakable and learn more about our shadow selves.

'Stick and stones can break my bones but words can never hurt me,' is something Irish parents used to say when coaching their children in the ways of the world. At its core is a message of passive resistance and resilience. It was a commonly used phrase in different contexts, and for some in the early years of the Free State words were recognised as having power, and power was to be acquired and exercised by the select few over the many. Control of language and words became crucial to the success of the Church–State alliance forged during the first decades of the Free State.

The effect was one of silencing and oppression, and in that space where words are caged and expression and questioning executed, fear and despair grows. We were told it was 'God's will' and were directed to 'Offer everything up to the Sacred Heart of Jesus' and his bleeding heart.

As their daughters were about to transition to menstruating and adolescence, mothers of Ireland struggled to name it and explain it – the blood, the pains, the potential for pregnancy and the mystery of childbirth.

Diarmaid Ferriter writes:

> Although there was occasional reference to the need for
> young people to be better educated about sex and repro-
> duction, there were significant barriers in the way of this
> becoming widespread. Archbishop McQuaid, for exam-
> ple, found any public airing of issues to do with the female
> body and reproduction distasteful. In 1944 he contacted
> Conor Ward, secretary of the Department of Local Gov-
> ernment and Public Health, to inform him of a meeting
> of the Irish Hierarchy at which 'I explained very fully the
> evidence concerning the use of internal sanitary tampons,
> in particular that called Tampax. On the medical evidence
> made available, the bishops very strongly disapproved of
> the use of these appliances, more particularly in the case of
> unmarried persons'.[1]

As a school girl in the late 1970s, I recall that taboo material
not for general consumption included a book titled *Everywoman*,
written by Derek Llewllyn Jones. At the time it was secretly regarded among teenage girls as *the source* for information on the
anatomy and biology of females and provided educational content on reproduction, pregnancy and birth. Paging through it, I
am reminded of a brave male teacher who stood in front of thirty
uniformed girls about to graduate from secondary school in 1980.
He locked the door of the convent classroom and, using the over-
head projector, presented acetate slides on how babies are made
and born. He knew he was breaking the taboo, and we did too.

This courageous event took place fifty years after the 1929
Censorship of Publication Act, which provided for the banning
of books. In the decades that followed, as John Cooney explains,

. . . . the censorship system had banned writers of the stature of James Joyce, Sean O'Casey, Sigmund Freud, Thomas Mann, Graham Greene, H.G. Wells, George Bernard Shaw, Seán Ó'Faoláin, Frank O'Connor, Liam O'Flaherty, Kate O'Brien, Oliver St John Gogarty, Bertrand Russell, George Orwell, Noel Coward, W. Somerset Maughan, Ernest Hemingway, Truman Capote, William Faulkner, F. Scott Fitzgerald, Margaret Mead, Marcel Proust, Jean-Paul Sartre, André Gide and Simone de Beauvoir. This system, supported wholeheartedly by McQuaid, was described by Paul Blanshard as offering 'honourable dishonour' to the banned writers.[2]

The influence of McQuaid on cultural oppression is well illustrated by this reference:

When a UCD student, Michael Gorman, visited Séan O'Casey at Totnes in Devon during 1950, he asked why he wouldn't come back to Ireland, where he was assured of a warm reception from a younger generation, who regarded him as one of their great models. O'Casey told Gorman, 'I shall never come back to Ireland, as long as the arch-druid of Drumcondra is alive'.[3]

He was referring to Archbishop John Charles McQuaid, who supported 'the wholesale clean-up of evil literature' and was assisted in this crusade by the Knights of Saint Columbanus. In 1950:

Supreme Knight, Stephen McKenzie obtained the Archbishop's support for an action plan to set up 'committees of readers' to visit libraries and bookshops to inspect and read free of charge any of the books available to the public. In cases where librarians or shop keepers refused to grant the 'readers' these facilities, they were to be reported to the Knights' HQ at Ely Place. Readers were urged to send pornographic books or periodicals to the secretary of the Censorship of Publications Board, with a covering note outlining the offensive passages. Many public library books went missing or pages were defaced at the hands of the holy snoopers.[4]

Attempts to introduce a health and welfare education and support scheme to mothers and children met resistance at a time when doctors were expressing concern about malnutrition and persistent poverty. Ferriter writes that in 1986, Noël Browne, who served as Minister for Health between 1948 and 1951, published his memoir *Against the Tide*, in which he

. . . castigates the actions of the clergy in blocking his proposed Mother and Child Scheme in 1951: 'I was left with a clear impression that the Church thrived on mass illiteracy and that the welfare of care in the bodily sense of the bulk of our people was a secondary consideration to the need to maintain the religious ethos in the health service.'[5]

> *Patriarchy depends on the mother to act as a conservative influence, imprinting future adults with patriarchal values even in those early years when the mother–child relationship might seem most individual and private; it has also assured through ritual and tradition that the mother shall cease, at a certain point, to hold the child – in particular the son – in her orbit. Certainly it has created images of the archetypal Mother which reinforce the conservatism of motherhood and convert it to an energy for the renewal of male power.'*

Adrienne Rich[6]

The control of access to information and alternative viewpoints remained a focus for Church–State engagement for decades. Ferriter refers to research on the period and writes that, in the 1960s:

Father Thomas Finnegan, a priest of the Diocese of Elphin, published a pamphlet with the Catholic Truth Society of Ireland, entitled *Questions Young Women Ask. . .* As Finnegan's analysis moved from its doomladen main section to its blunt and negative conclusion that passionate kissing was 'mortally sinful' for the unmarried, he came up with suggestions as to how the wholesome girl could keep lustful thoughts at bay:

Do not think about your 'bad thoughts'. Say quickly 'Jesus save me – Mary help me' and then think of something else. If you are a domestic sort of girl, picture to yourself the little house that you and your future husband are going to live in and decide on the colour schemes for the various rooms . . . or, if you are the athletic type of girl, pretend to yourself that an uncle has given you money to buy a car with. By the time you have decided between the relative merits of a Morris Minor or a Ford Anglia, the bad thoughts will be forgotten.[7]

Cooney further tells us:

> In July [1967] the Government decided to remove a ban on
> books that had been proscribed for more than 12 years –
> some 5,000 titles in all. However, it decided not to amend
> laws banning the sale of contraceptives 'until the moral
> problems are clarified for Catholics'. In a memorandum to
> the Government, Lenihan [Minister for Justice] based his
> case on a liberalisation of the law in Britain, where D.H.
> Lawrence's *Lady Chatterley's Lover* was declared not to be
> obscene on the grounds that a person might not be con-
> victed if it was proved that publication was for the public
> good and in the interests of science, art or literature.[8]

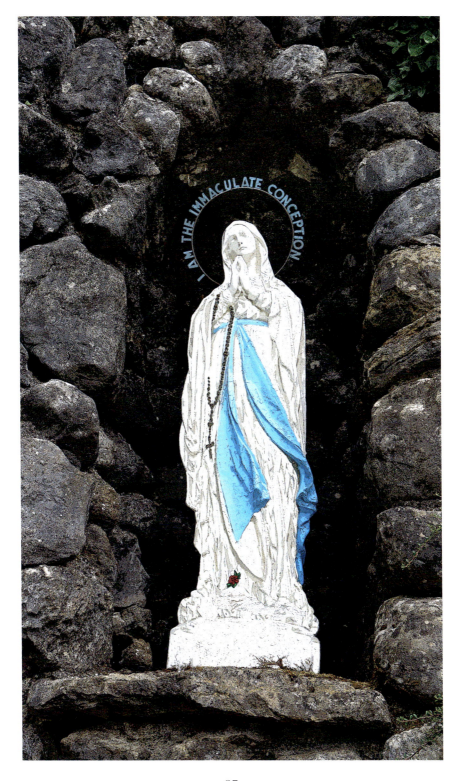

In my memory, it was the 1970s and the weekly arrival from England of *The Sun* newspaper with a topless female model on page three that began to widen the cracks in the dam of silence and control. This, along with membership of the European Economic Community and access to BBC radio and television, added to the testing of the boundaries of Church–State authority. Pirate radio stations broadcasting to the populace from ships offshore were energising the youth, along with the new ways of thinking brought back to Ireland, by emigrants of earlier years. These voices began to stretch viewpoints and freedom of expression. Among the loudest voices was Bob Geldof and the Boomtown Rats with their hit 'Banana Republic' in 1980.

It was not until the 1990s that the tsunami of truths of sadistic and systemic abuse by clergy and religious orders, which began as a trickle, became unstoppable and has under-pinned a complete transformation in Irish life.

From the other side of the planet in Australia in 1990, the news that Mary Robinson was elected as the first female president of the Ireland stirred in me a sense of hope and possibility that 'maybe one day I could return to live there?' When she thanked the women of Ireland for coming out to vote, I thought, 'maybe, finally, the silencing has passed and the voice of women is beginning to make waves?'

6.

The Banished Children of Eve

It was a time when parents who abused their children were simply called 'strict', when the spiritual lacerations of profoundly exploited women were referred to as 'nervous breakdowns', when girls and women who were tightly girdled, tightly reined and tightly muzzled were called 'nice', and those other females who managed to slip the collar for a moment or two of life were branded 'bad'.

Clarissa Pinkola Estés[1]

Hail, Holy Queen, mother of mercy, hail, our life,
our sweetness and our hope. To thee do we cry, poor
banished children of Eve: to thee do we send up our
sighs, mourning and weeping in this valley of tears.

Turn then most gracious advocate, thine eyes of mercy
towards us, and after this our exile, show unto us the
blessed fruit of thy womb, Jesus. O clement, O loving,
O sweet Virgin Mary! Do not reject my petition but
graciously hear and answer it. Amen.

Hail Holy Queen prayer

Why Banish Eve?

When our mothers were on their knees praying for the 'Banished Children of Eve', most of us never knew who these people were. They existed somewhere out there, out of sight but not always out of harm's way. As the decades rumbled by, the 'Banished Children of Eve' have emerged from the dark shadows of Irish society. At times they have become the focus of government-commissioned investigations and reports.

It has been revealed that the 'Banished Children of Eve' are the children abused in secret by their families, while many people suspected it but remained silent. They are the children abused by members of religious orders and institutions while authorities acquiesced and society was tightly controlled. They are the women who were declared to be of 'unsound mind' and locked in the 'madhouse' for simply being inconvenient. They are the children abandoned by the state to become victims of endless, brutal and soul-destroying abuse at the hands of sadistic authority figures. They are the unmarried mothers who took

the boat to England as rejected, penniless women, and saw out their days in factories, the prisons or on the streets. They are the women who moved to other lands without their 'illegitimate' babies and went on to marry and become a mother to others, all the while carrying a secret past around in a broken heart. They are the unmarried mothers confined to Magdalen Laundries, often for their lifetime. They are the children who were overlooked, boarded-out or exported by a compliant state while those responsible hid behind the lace curtains of religious institutions and non-existent or questionable legal and regulatory pathways.

Sprinkled through the pages that follow are spoonfuls of doctrine from the pages of *A Catechism of Catholic Doctrine* (1951). The contents of that little book formed the basis of instruction, control and engagement of the entire Catholic population of Ireland during the decades that followed the establishment of the Irish Free State in 1922.

The little 'Catechism book' was a staple requirement of every Catholic child's school bag, and rote learning of the content was mandatory for participation in the sacrament of confirmation at the age of eleven or twelve.

It is worth remembering that most children finished their education at fourteen or younger, and only the privileged or those who won scholarships were afforded second level education, thereby restricting opportunities for society as a whole to benefit from reading, debating and integrating other viewpoints.

This remained the case until free second level education was introduced in Ireland in 1967. It is also worth remembering that, in the decades prior to 1967, approximately 5,000 books were banned for sale or distribution within the wider society.

> *Did Adam and Eve obey the command of God?*
> *Adam and Eve did not obey the command of God:*
> *they were tempted by the devil, and ate the forbidden fruit.*[2]

Given that over ninety per cent of the population of the Irish Free State, then the Republic of Ireland, were Roman Catholic during the decades 1922–1986, and that every Sunday saw the majority of the population attend Mass (as failure to do so was a 'mortal sin'), inclusion of doctrine within this essay assists with clarifying the 'mindset' of the population. For decades Irish society hid from public gaze their unwed pregnant daughters, sisters and lovers and their unclaimed offspring and newly born relatives.

> *What is scandal?*
> *By scandal is meant any word, act or omission,*
> *which tends to lead another into sin.*[3]

As this chapter unfolds, segments of apologies and statements made on behalf of the State are included. These segments acknowledge the existence of the many institutions that contained women and children. The words spoken in the Dáil recognise the traumatic impact cultural judgement has had and continues to have on their lives. Speaking in response to the content of the 'Commission of Investigation into Mother and Baby Homes' (CIMBH), Tánaiste Leo Varadkar observed:

As the report shows, this was a stifling, oppressive and deeply misogynistic culture. It was a cold house for most of its people for most of its existence.[4]

Was any human person ever preserved from original sin? The Blessed Virgin Mary, Mother of God, was preserved free from original sin, and this privilege is called her Immaculate Conception.[5]

Adam and Eve Meet Church and State

In her chapter in *Motherhood in Ireland*, Patricia Burke Brogan writes:

The image of Eve as the seducer of man and the sinner who lost the Garden of Paradise for all humanity, cast its shadow over women's lives. Deep within that shadow we find the Magdalene Home Laundries [and Mother and Baby Homes]. From the time of the Potato Famine until the early 1970s, the 'fallen women' of Ireland, unmarried mothers, who had broken the sixth or ninth commandments, scrubbed society's dirty clothes. Betrayed by lovers, signed in by families or guardians, they lived a spartan and loveless existence.[6]

Varadkar stated:

This report shames Irish society entirely. Women pregnant outside of marriage, some very young, some the victims of rape, were not supported by their families, communities or by fathers of their children. They turned to the church and State for refuge. While they got refuge, it was a cold and often cruel one. Church and State ran these homes together, operating hand in glove, equally culpable, doing so with the full knowledge, acquiescence and even support of wider society.[7]

> *What is forbidden by the sixth commandment?*
> *The sixth commandment forbids not only adultery, but all*
> *looks, words and actions against the virtue of chastity.*[8]

Taoiseach Enda Kenny made a statement in the Dáil on 19 February 2013:

> The Magdalene women might have been told that they were washing away a wrong or a sin, but we know now and to our shame they were only ever scrubbing away our nation's shadow... We now know that the State itself was directly involved in over a quarter of all admissions to the Magdalene laundries, be it through the social services, reformatories, psychiatric institutions, county homes, the prison and probation services and industrial schools.[9]

Pregnant unmarried girls and women had little choice in Ireland, and many took the boat to England. In the mid-1950s, increased immigration of young pregnant women into England influenced priests, charities and local government services there to request changes in Ireland. As their voices reached a crescendo, the Irish hierarchy and government authorities considered a ban on young women travelling and repatriation of some women who were 'POA' (pregnant on arrival) and had their baby in England.

In his book *Occasions of Sin*, Diarmaid Ferriter, writes:

> Father Tom Fitzgerald, a native of Tipperary and prison chaplain in some of the toughest parishes in the East End of London, was reported in the *Standard* newspaper as insisting 'the self-righteousness of the Irish is the cause of the trouble. Our people at home do not face the fact that there is original sin in Ireland as much as in any other part of the world ... nine out of ten people who go wrong here

were wrong before they set foot on England's shore … a girl who goes wrong in England was restrained at home only by outward conventions, not by faith, not by anything deep within herself.'[10]

During the decades before and after the establishment of the Irish Free State in 1922, the following values were promoted in family and community life: transition of land from father to son, preservation of the 'good name' of the family and the cultural belief that when a woman married, she became one dimension of the chattel of her husband. This set of values placed the father as 'head of the household' and largely responsible for placement of the 'offending' daughter outside the family and community circle. This was reinforced through the fundamental principles of Bunreacht na h'Éireann, which underpinned legislation on matters relating to marriage, gendered roles and property ownership and succession. These structures supported a deeply patriarchal society and became a powerful force for the containment and silencing of women and their 'illegitimate' children.

As Hope Edelman writes:

> A father is a daughter's first heterosexual interest, and her relationship with him becomes the most influential blueprint for her later attachments to men. Throughout a daughter's childhood and adolescence, she picks up clues from her father about how to relate to males. Though it may sound implausible at first, given what we know about same-sex modeling, some of a girl's *feminine* identifications come from having a father who exhibits the traditionally *masculine* traits of instrumentalism and assertion. Fathers also tend to reinforce sex-typed behaviour in their daughters, subtly urging them to conform to behaviours and play that emphasize caretaking and cooperation.[11]

Absent Men, Absent Mothers and Abandoned Eve

Internationally, the natural 'way of things' is for a pregnant girl or woman to seek the support of female relatives, mothers, sisters or aunts. For women and girls who were also first-time mothers, the experience of being dispatched to an institution for an indefinite period and without any reference to what is understood in our time as 'informed consent', must have elicited intense feelings of rejection, fear and abandonment.

Hope Edelman observes:

> The mother who abandons her daughter leaves a pile of questions behind: Who was she? Who is she? Where is she? Why did she leave? Her presence created the daughter's life, but her absence defines it. Like the child whose mother dies, the abandoned daughter lives with a loss, but

she also struggles with the knowledge that her mother is alive yet inaccessible and out of touch. Death has a finality to it that abandonment does not.[12]

> *What is forbidden by the ninth commandment?*
> *The ninth commandment forbids all deliberate pleasure in*
> *impure thoughts, and all deliberate consent to impure desires.*[13]

The report of the CIMBH examined the history of Mother and Baby Homes and found they 'were not unique to Ireland; in fact, Ireland was a latecomer but they did remain in existence for longer than other countries'.[14]

Of particular interest within the report is the statement that:

> Catholics appear to have been slow to establish mother and baby homes, perhaps because members of the female religious orders were precluded from involvement in childbirth.[15]

When played out in practice this meant that unmarried pregnant girls and women who were placed in the monastic-style setting of a Magdalen Laundry or Mother and Baby Home, often found themselves entirely alone when giving birth.

The report explains that, by the end of the nineteenth century,

> . . . special facilities for unmarried mothers were provided by charities, not by the state. Mother and baby homes were seen as places where women could be redeemed and offered the opportunity to repent and do penance for their 'sin' by working and praying. Redemption and religious practice were seen as an integral part of the care and 'rehabilitation' of unmarried mothers, by Protestant and Catholic charities alike.[16]

Irish women knew that:

> An illegitimate birth could destroy the marriage prospects, not just for the woman who had given birth, but for her siblings, hence the pressures to keep it a secret by sending her to a mother and baby home. Many women who concealed their pregnancy from parents or family were conscious of such attitudes. Pressure to keep their pregnancy secret added to a woman's trauma.[17]

This led young women into a situation where childbirth became a crisis for many of the entrants to Magdalen Laundries and Mother and Baby Homes.

Once women were admitted, the structures of institutional life added to the experience of rejection and depersonalisation. The sense of collective 'guilt' of the group of 'penitents' promoted a detachment from individual identity and personal history. The women

> . . . were dissuaded from sharing their stories with their fellow residents because of concerns to protect their privacy though such conversations might have offered some comfort at a traumatic time. Conditions improved in all respects in the later decades.[18]

In his statement to the Dáil following the publication of the report of the CIMBH, the Taoiseach, Micheál Martin, said:

> This report reveals the dominant role of the churches and their moral code and lays bare the failures of the State.[19]

Research presented by Ferriter in *Occasions of Sin* reveals that, while empathy was evident in the corridors of power, action and a respect for human rights and equality was not reflected in the language of government. Ferriter refers to a 'memorandum for the Department of the Taoiseach' in which

> . . . there was a degree of charitable thinking, perhaps even sympathy towards unmarried mothers: 'Many unfortunate unmarried mothers are denied the shelter of their own families and it is possible that some of them, who might otherwise reform, drift into the prostitute class in a spirit of despair induced by the hardships they suffer. It can be readily appreciated that girls of the domestic

servant class who get into difficulty find themselves in a position of great hardship trying to earn their living and to maintain an illegitimate child away from their ordinary place of work. A weekly contribution from the father of the child would ease this situation considerably. It is not impossible too, that the ability to obtain an affiliation order may lessen the number of cases of infanticide.'[20]

The CIMBH reports that in 1928 Father Richard Devane, wrote:

> Here is an opportunity for nuns to exercise Christ-like charity towards their weak and unfortunate little sisters, to raise them up to virtue and self-respect, and save them from drifting further down the road to ruin. . . . It is further suggested that relief to unmarried mothers must have as a condition their being willing to agree to be detained, in case of a first offender for twelve months, of second offender two years . . .[21]

Eve, Her Child and the Institution

> It was also suggested that a first-time mother should remain with her child and feed her child until the infant was approximately one year old. This was often viewed as an integral part of the woman's rehabilitation. Requiring a mother to care for her child at least until the infant was weaned, for perhaps a year, would give her a sense of maternal responsibility that would deter her from another pregnancy and perhaps encourage her to contribute to her child's upkeep.[22]

In addition to unmarried mothers, Magdalen Laundries served as a means for containing women who were seen to be 'offenders' by the courts. The broad categories through which criminal justice referrals occurred were Remand, Probation, Courts, Prison and An Garda Síochána. The 2013 report of the 'Inter-departmental Committee to establish the facts of State involvement with the Magdalen Laundries' (also known as the McAleese Report) states that:

Taken together, these categories of referrals amounted to 8.1 per cent of known entries to the Magdalen Laundries. The youngest girl known to have entered a Magdalen Laundry by one of these routes was 11, while the oldest was 60.[23]

Behind the statistics is an awareness of risk to girls and young women, including sexual abuse. Ferriter highlights that:

> Child sexual abuse simply was not prioritised as an area worthy of immediate political and social action as pointed out by Moira Maguire: 'Far from being ignorant of the vulnerability of children to sexual abuse in the first half of the twentieth century, lawmakers, jurists and the public of the period were in general well aware of the problem, even if there was little public comment . . . in the government's response to sexual assaults against children, the poor, disaffected, and marginalised were sacrificed to the "greater good" – which in this case meant male sexual licence and protecting the newly independent state's legitimacy and reputation in the international arena.'[24]

> *Why are we obliged to keep secrets?*
> *We are obliged to keep secrets because the interest*
> *of our neighbour and the public good require it.*[25]

> *How are we to obey our parents?*
> *We are to obey our parents while under their care by doing*
> *readily what they command, provided it not be sinful.*[26]

Containing Eve and Her Offspring

The report of the CIMBH states that:

> Women were brought to mother and baby homes by their parents or other family members without being consulted as to their destination. . . . There is no evidence that women were forced to enter mother and baby homes by church or State authorities. Most women had no alternative.[27]

The McAleese Report found that, on examining the records on the next of kin, 'In 5,490 cases' of the girls and women admitted to Magdalen Laundries, 'no information was included on family background'. This equated to '49 per cent of the relevant dataset'.[28]

The report of the CIMBH states that:

> It is commonly believed and has been widely stated on numerous occasions that women were required to remain in a mother and baby home for two years after the birth of their child. This was never a legal requirement although

. . . many women appear to have believed it was. The
motivation behind the two-year stay was both moral and
pragmatic: a belief, that two years was sufficient time to
'reform' or 'rehabilitate' a woman.[29]

Funding to support the Mother and Baby Homes came from
a variety of sources.

> The overwhelming majority of women and children were
> maintained in the institutions by their local authority but
> there were some who were 'private patients' and were
> paid for by themselves or family members. In many cases,
> they were cut off from the world and some were assigned
> a 'house name'. The mother and baby homes gave women
> some assurance that their secret would be protected.[30]

The report of the CIMBH states that:

While mother and baby homes were not a peculiarly Irish phenomenon, the proportion of Irish unmarried mothers who were admitted to mother and baby homes or county homes in the twentieth century was probably the highest in the world.[31]

The report also reveals that:

There were about 56,000 unmarried mothers and about 57,000 children in mother and baby homes and county homes investigated by the Commission … and it is likely that there were a further 25,000 unmarried mothers and a larger number of children in the county homes which were not investigated; admissions to county homes were largely pre-1960.[32]

Again, Hope Edelmann helps us to understand the emotional turmoil the women and girls may have experienced:

When a daughter's assumptions about the world as a safe, nurturing place are shattered in an instant she has to re-structure her beliefs and rebuild some of her faith before she can devote much energy to confronting her mother's absence. We mourn only when we feel stable and secure enough to relinquish some control – not when we're antic-ipating another blow from behind.[33]

What is actual sin?
Actual sin is the sin which we ourselves commit
by any wilful thought, word, deed or omission
contrary to the law of God.[34]

The records of mother and baby homes and government files almost always describe unmarried mothers as 'girls'. This terminology was common in Ireland and internationally.[35]

The use of the word 'girls' suggests immaturity and requiring supervision, thereby reinforcing the belief that unmarried pregnant women were 'less able' or were 'victims' or 'sinners'. Ferriter writes:

> One-third of the 'street' girls dealt with at the Legion of Mary hostel in Harcourt Street were ex-industrial school girls, according to a communication with the Department of Health in 1950 from Frank Duff. one of the few men who opposed the use of these schools.[36]

Their admission to the hostel from a background of industrial schools suggests homelessness and destitution and the inherent risks of that experience. Ferriter explains that

> . . . the court archive would suggest there was also a belief that teenage girls were more responsible than their male assailants for sexual assaults [thereby contributing to] concerns that girls would blackmail men [and reflecting the court process as having] a regard for the 'reputation of innocent men' and more preoccupation with the 'character' of females than males.[37]

The report of the CIMBH states that:

> The women who were admitted to mother and baby homes ranged in age from 12 years old to women in their forties. However, 80 per cent were aged between 18 and 29 years and this was remarkably consistent across the larger mother and baby homes. 5,616 women, 11.4 per cent of the total for whom information about their age is available, were under 18 years of age. The Commission has not seen evidence that the Gardaí [police] were routinely notified about pregnancies in under-age women.[38]

The stated primary mission of these homes was to promote reform and repentance though they also rescued destitute women from homelessness and life on the streets. It was widely believed that many first-time unmarried mothers became prostitutes and went on to give birth to additional 'illegitimate' children. If first-time mothers spent time in homes cut off from the world, carrying out domestic duties, being trained for future employment in domestic work, caring for their child, and spending time in prayer and other religious experiences, it was believed that they would avoid that danger.[39]

When is a sin mortal?
A sin is mortal when the act is grievously wrong,
and is committed with clear knowledge and full consent.[40]

In her book *Motherless Daughters*, Hope Edelman observes that:

> Without knowledge of her own experiences, and their relationship to her mothers', a daughter is snipped from the female cord that connects the generations of women in her family, the feminine line of descent that Naomi Lowinsky calls the 'Motherline'. A woman achieves her psychic connection to generations of feminine wisdom through hearing her mother's and grandmothers' narratives about women's physical, psychological, and historical changes – bleeding, birthing, suckling, aging and dying, Dr Lowinsky says: 'When a woman today comes to

understand her life story as a story from the Motherline, she gains female authority in a number of ways. First, her Motherline grounds her in her feminine nature as she struggles with the many options now open to women. Second, she reclaims carnal knowledge of her own body, its blood mysteries and their power. Third, as she makes the journey back to her female roots, she will encounter ancestors who struggled with similar difficulties in different historical times. This provides her with life-cycle perspective that softens her immediate situation.'[41]

What is servile work?
Servile work is that which requires labour
of body rather than of mind.[42]

Eve Earns Her Keep in a World Without End

The report of the CIMBH states that:

> The workload for the women in county homes was of a dif-
> ferent magnitude to the mother and baby homes. Unmar-
> ried mothers were far outnumbered by children, including
> older children, and by elderly and incapacitated adults.
> Most county homes did not employ domestic staff so un-
> married women were assigned onerous duties that were
> essential to the running of these homes. There are many
> contemporary statements by local officials or matrons
> insisting that unmarried mothers could not be removed
> from the county home, because there would be nobody to
> carry out this work. A lack of hot water and sanitary facil-
> ities, the old, dilapidated buildings, with stone staircases
> and corridors, made their work even more difficult and
> unpleasant.[43]

County homes accommodated adults and children with special needs who would have required extra assistance and personal care. Women continued to carry out unpaid work in some county homes until the early 1960s, despite a statement by the Minister of Health in 1952 that this was prohibited.[44]

What the state and society availed of were the unpaid services of alienated women, whose voices were silenced and experiences ignored. The residents of county homes were often the intellectually disabled, the infirm and people with severe physical and psychological difficulties. In addition to the housekeeping tasks of changing soiled beds and clothing, cooking and cleaning, the unpaid carers would have attended to the toileting, feeding and heavy lifting needs of the most disabled persons.

How did God punish the angels who rebelled?
God punished the angels who rebelled by
condemning them to the everlasting pains of hell.[45]

Women whose testimony contributed to the McAleese Report explained that they had no details of how long they were to be confined to a Magdalen Laundry, and this persistent sense of not knowing underpinned a life-long anxiety.

The Report of the Interdepartmental Committee explains that:

> Due to this lack of information and the fact that they had been placed in an institution among many older women, a large number of women spoke of a very real fear that they would remain in the Magdalen Laundry for the rest of their lives. Even if they left the laundries after a very short time, some women told the committee that they were never able to fully free themselves of this fear and uncertainty.[46]

> The confusion and hurt experienced by these women when placed in a Magdalen Laundry was, undoubtedly, exacerbated by the fact that they had absolutely no idea why they were there. For many of them, this also meant that on leaving the Magdalen Laundry, they were fearful that, for some unknown reason, they might be brought back there again.[47]

> Some of the women told the Committee that they felt free of this fear only after they left Ireland to live abroad.[48]

There were some women within the Magdalen Laundries who were described as 'Auxillaries'. They were also referred to as 'Magdalens' or 'Consecrates', and the McAleese Report states these were names applied to women who chose to remain confined to the Magdalen Laundry for life.[49]

The process of 'informed consent' as we understand it today seems absent from the research.

What should one do when tempted by impure
thoughts or desires? A person tempted by impure thoughts
or desires should at once pray for grace to resist them,
turn his mind to good thoughts and occupy
himself with useful activities.[50]

The report of the CIMBH states that:

The average number of women in Sean Ross [Abbey] and Castlepollard in the early 1950s was 140 or higher and the large size inevitably meant that Irish mother and baby homes were impersonal and highly regimented.[51]

Silenced Eve and Rigid Institutions

Interviews with members of one religious congregation who contributed to the McAleese Report noted that:

> Until the 1970s life in the refuge [Magdalene Laundry] was influenced by the monastic routine. The residents normally began their day with Mass, followed by breakfast, then work. Dinner was served at 12.30pm and tea at 6pm. What was termed 'recreation time' followed the midday and evening meals. Periods of prayer were observed during the day. The following were the practices:

- The rosary was recited during the working day – called out by a resident or Sister to which all responded as they worked

- There was a pause for the Angelus at 12.00 and 6pm

- The Sacred Heart prayer was recited at 4pm.

Within these specific prayer times, silence was observed.[52]

Why didn't our mothers and great-grandmothers tell us what battle it was we lost, or never fought, so that we would understand how total was our defeat, and that religion and madness and frigidity were how we mourned it?

Why were our mothers so silent about rape and incest and prostitution and their own lack of pleasure? Why, when they had so many words, did they not name our heroines for us, tell us about feminists and suffragists and Amazons and great-mothers?

Phyllis Chesler[53]

The report of the CIMBH states that:

The length of time that women stayed in Irish mother and baby homes was linked to the provision of a long-term placement for the children, and the fact that legal adoption was not introduced until 1953. Unmarried mothers were legally responsible for their children. A mother could not leave a mother and baby home or a county home without taking her child or until long-term arrangements had been made for the child. Local authorities were unwilling to take responsibility for the children of unmarried mothers until they were at least two years old, and often older . . .

Some women were required to remain in a county home, working without pay, in return for their child being boarded out by the local authority. . . . There is evidence that in counties Wexford and Meath (and perhaps other counties), women who sought to leave the county home were presented with their child, who had been removed from a foster home, and told that they were responsible for the child's upkeep.[54]

To capture the emotional pain experienced by women and children who endured this regime is a challenge. In her 2004 article, 'To Enliven Her Was My Living', Fiona Gardner, references a poem written by D.W. Winnicott, titled 'The Tree'. Winnicott was considered a pioneer in the study of parent-child attachment. His words, which are said to reflect memories of his own mother, may touch on the experience of many women and children who survived these institutions.

Mother below is weeping,
     weeping
     weeping
Thus I knew her
Once stretched out on her lap
  as now on dead tree
I learned to make her smile
  to stem her tears
  to undo her guilt
  to cure her inward death
To enliven her was my living.[55]

The CIMBH report continues:

The statistics reveal a significant discrepancy between private and public patients. Private patients, or more probably their families, could afford to pay for the child to be placed at nurse [foster care], or as frequently happened in the 1940s, for the child to remain in Bessborough [a mother and baby home in County Cork] without their mother, under the auspices of the Catholic Women's Aid Society. However, a majority of public patients left mother and baby homes within a year of the birth of their child. This suggests that the women or their family made financial arrangements for the long-term care of their child. A number of witnesses spoke of the Sisters being paid a sum of money to buy a mother's 'release'; this money was used to place her child 'at nurse' generally through an intermediary charitable society.[56]

The longest stays were among women who lacked financial and personal support from their family that would enable them to make arrangements for their child. A number of women who were admitted to Bessborough in the 1920s remained there for the rest of their lives.[57]

What are fast days?
Fast days are days on which we are
allowed only one full meal.[58]

Hunger or Death for Eve and the Infants

In 1941, rationing was introduced across the country. This determined a person's access to food, clothing and other supplies. Also that year, a Department of Local Government and Public Health survey 'suggested 60 per cent of Dublin mothers were unable to breastfeed on account of their own malnourishment'.[59]

Families living in overcrowded conditions in Dublin's inner city and in working-class housing areas were in dire need during the Emergency years (1939–45),

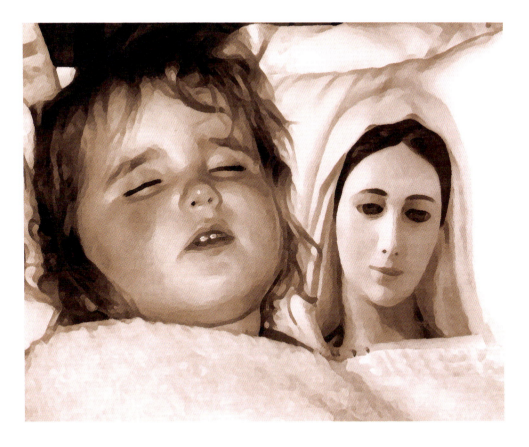

. . . to the extent that the government had to introduce sup-
plemented food allowances in September 1941. . . . Lack of
amenities for children, poor living conditions and general
nutritional problems meant that they were hit badly by TB
and rickets (in 1943 an estimated of 173 per 1,000 children
were suffering from some form of rickets).[60]

Also in Dublin:

In 1938, 111,950 people were living in 6,307 tenement
houses, half of which were reckoned incurably unfit for
habitation.[61]

Some other stark statistics of the time, recorded by Ferriter in *The Transformation of Ireland, 1900–2000*, reflect the extent of poverty and desperation:

> In 1939 the overall infant and child mortality rates per 1,000 of the population of the Irish Free State was 66; for the Dublin County Borough it was 90. Death rates from TB per 1,000 of the population in the same year were 1.13 nationally, but 1.48 in Dublin. . . . As late as 1945, a report of the TB committee established by the government noted that practical problems such as unpasteurised milk had still not been tackled, and claimed that Dublin slums were littered with crippled children because they were drinking contaminated milk and enduring overcrowding while living at or below the poverty limit.[62]

Prior to the escalating crisis evident amongst the working class during the Emergency years there was still residue of categorising 'the deserving poor' and 'the undeserving poor' by society and by those who were in the position of distributing aid and food to those in need. The 'undeserving poor' were seen to have somehow contributed to their impoverishment through

immoral or slothful behaviours. The introduction of supplemen-
tal food allowances in September 1941 'was frowned upon by
some Catholic activists, who resented this "interference" with
the family, a foretaste of some of the rancorous debates which
were to follow',[63] including over Dr Noël Browne's Mother and
Child Scheme.

At this time of crisis in Irish life, Cooney writes that Archbishop McQuaid

> . . . called on the Government, public authorities, educa-
> tionalists, charity and social workers 'to make it their first
> concern to appreciate the vast riches of the treasury of
> our Faith, with its divinely given remedies for all our so-
> cial life'. Catholics were to accept in a spirit of obedience
> the censorship and food-rationing measures which 'the
> Supreme Civil Authority' found it necessary to ordain.[64]

Early in 1941, McQuaid 'invited 40 Catholic organisations
to the Mansion House' – which 'led to the formation of a provisional body to draw up proposals to alleviate poverty in the
city'.[65] This was later to be known as the Catholic Social Service
Conference (CSSC).

In mid-March the planning group met for two days… and set about exploring solutions to the crisis developing in Dublin and elsewhere.

A number of initiatives arose from this collective approach.

Most ambitiously of all, the conference proposed setting up five large communal food and fuel distributing centres in Dublin, which would cater for about 500 families in each district.[66]

Ferriter writes that the CSSC 'ran 27 food centres in Dublin supplying 250,000 meals per month'.[67]

What are days of abstinence?
Days of abstinence are days on which we are
forbidden the use of flesh-meat and its products.[68]

The report of the CIMBH states that:

There is some evidence that food in mother and baby homes may have been inadequate during the Emergency years. A diet served to mothers in Bessborough [Mother and Baby Home in Cork] on a 'fast' day in 1943 appears to have been seriously deficient in protein but there is no information regarding the quantities.[69]

As ration books were introduced to Magdalen Laundries and Mother and Baby Homes:

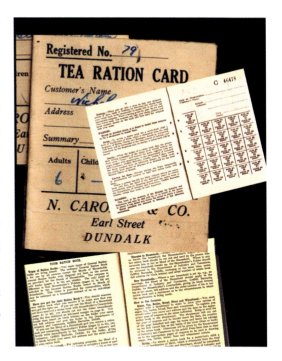

> Heads of institutions were instructed to retain their ration books for: 'inmates' . . . as long as they are resident in the institution. When an inmate is leaving, the address to which he is going should be inserted on his book which should then be handed to him.

By contrast, ration books for 'members of resident staff' could be either retained by the manager or provided to those individuals.[70]

In the years 1935–45, the

> . . . chance of a child born in a mother and baby home surviving until their first birthday, was just over half of that of an 'illegitimate' child who was not in a mother and baby home. The adverse impact of mother and baby homes lessened in the next decade: in the years 1946–55, mother and baby homes accounted for 39.6 per cent of deaths of 'illegitimate' children and 30.5 per cent of births. By the 1960s infant mortality in mother and baby homes was equal to, or lower than, the national rate for 'illegitimate' children.[71]

The report of the CIMBH found that:

Infant mortality rates peaked in most homes during the early and mid-1940s coinciding with a national peak in infant mortality. 75 per cent of children born in Bessborough in 1943 died within the first year of life, 62 per cent of children born that year in the Bethany Home died. The high infant mortality raised serious questions about mother and baby homes: the large size, unqualified staff and inadequate staffing, poor management, and the limitations on the local and national authorities' willingness and capacity to implement reforms.[72]

Deputy Roderic O'Gorman made a statement in the Dáil on 13 January 2021:

Alice Litster was an inspector for the Department of Local Government from 1927 to 1957. The commission's report states that Ms Litster tried valiantly to have conditions in the institutions improved. It was Ms Litster who wrote the first criticism of mother and baby homes by a civil servant, criticisms that were subsequently watered down by departmental officials. It is from her reports on the institutions that much of the commission's information about them in the decades after independence is drawn. She highlighted the high number of children being sent for adoption in the US. The report makes clear the acts of responsibility from those in power were notable for their rarity, particularly in the early days of the State.[73]

Where did Christ's soul go after his death?
After Christ's death his soul descended into hell:
this was not the hell of the damned, but a place
or state of rest called limbo.[74]

The CIMBH report also states that:

> The high rate of infant mortality (first year of life) in Irish
> mother and baby homes is probably the most disquieting
> feature of these institutions… about 9,000 children died
> in the institutions under investigation – approximately 15
> per cent of all children who were in the institutions… It is
> particularly disquieting that the high mortality rate was
> known to the authorities both local and national and was
> even described in public reports.[75]

There is no evidence of public concern being expressed about conditions in mother and baby homes or about the appalling mortality among the children born in these homes even though many of the facts were in the public domain . . . with the exception of memoranda written by Miss Litster and submissions by the Joint Committee of Women's Societies and Social Workers, proposing alternative arrangements for supporting unmarried mothers and their children, there is no indication that consideration was given to effecting major changes to existing provisions.[76]

With the decline in infant mortality in the late 1940s in the mother and baby homes and nationally, the motivation for major reforms abated and to pursue reforms 'would have involved fraught negotiations with religious congregations and members of the Catholic Hierarchy'.[77]

Who are in limbo?
The souls of the just who died before Christ
are in limbo, awaiting redemption.[78]

A conclusion reached by the CIMBH is that:

There is no single explanation for the appalling level of infant mortality in Irish mother and baby homes.[79]

Taoiseach Micheál Martin made a statement in the Dáil on 13 January 2021:

For much of the period covered by the commission [of Investigation into Mother and Baby Homes], women as a group and regardless of age or class, were systematically discriminated against in relation to employment, family law and social welfare, solely because of their gender . . . Children were similarly unequal, and none more so than

those who were cruelly labelled 'illegitimate'. I share deeply the commission's unequivocal view that the existence of the status of 'illegitimacy' until 1987 in this country, 'was an egregious breach of human rights'. This was a huge injustice and blighted the lives of many.[80]

Those who work with adults and children who have experienced profound loss and trauma, know there are times when words cannot be found to express the depth of emotional pain. At times such as these, the artistry of Percy Bysshe Shelley paints a picture familiar to many. Below is an extract from 'Stanzas Written in Dejection, near Naples'. It is said that the poet wrote these lines in December 1818, following a number of personal losses, including the death of his daughter, Clara, in childhood:

I could lie down like a tired child,
And weep away a life of care
Which I have borne and yet must bear,
Till death like sleep might steal on me,
And I might feel in the warm air
My cheek grow cold, and hear the sea
Breathe o'er my dying brain its last monotony.[81]

Eve and Her Infants – Scarred by Sin and State

The report of the CIMBH states:

> Attitudes towards unmarried mothers in Ireland reveal
> many similarities with those found elsewhere, but there
> were important differences. Irish families were less willing
> to provide a home and support to a daughter who had giv-
> en birth outside marriage and her child. This was due to a
> combination of factors – large families, poverty, but above
> all a concern with respectability, and a family's status in
> the community. In the late 1960s the number of unmarried
> mothers who kept their child was substantially lower and
> the proportion of 'illegitimate' babies who were adopted
> was substantially higher than elsewhere.[82]

> *Have we, the children of Adam, suffered because of his sin?*
> *Because of Adam's sin we are born without sanctifying grace,*
> *our intellect is darkened, our will is weakened, our passions*
> *incline us to evil and we are subject to suffering and death.*[83]

For the children who survived the institution of their birth,
the options for participation in society beyond the walls were
limited. Some children found themselves 'boarded out'. This was
a term used to describe 'foster care' arrangements, which facili-
tated handing over children to families who required assistance
on the farm, or a housekeeper or carer for a disabled or elderly
person or a companion who might be useful around the house
and yard. A monthly payment by the local council was often regarded as an addition to household income rather than financial
support to meet the needs of the child.

In his statement to the Dáil, Taoiseach Micheál Martin
stated:

Some children who were subsequently boarded out experienced heart-breaking exploitation, neglect and abuse within the families and communities in which they were placed. This was unforgiveable. The sense of abandonment felt by many of these children is palpable in the witness accounts. The circumstances of their birth, the arrangements for their early care, the stigma they experienced and the continuing lack of birth information is a terrible burden in their lives.[84]

Typical of the period were local and national newspapers reporting on attempts to apply 'attachment orders against putative fathers, and prosecutions for concealment of a birth or child neglect'. The local newspapers also contained 'extensive information about boarded out children'.

> Such stories should have been known to any regular reader of local newspapers and their circulation and readership was extensive.[85]

> When the Department of Health presented Galway County Council with a devastating report on the shortcomings of the boarding-out system in 1956, an editorial in the *Connacht Tribune* commented that: 'One would imagine that all members of Galway County Council would have been shocked by the report which was before them last Saturday regarding the conditions in which some children are boarded out by the Council. There were some expressions of indignation, but the reaction in a general way suggested that the Council were more annoyed with the case that cruelty could arise in a system that they as a council administered than that a number of children were exposed to the cruelty of neglect and indifference.'[86]

John Cooney identified that:

> In 1955 there were about 4,000 children in foster homes throughout the country, supervised by officers who had no specialised training in child care.[87]

In his statement to the Dáil, Deputy Alan Kelly said:

> All of us who serve in public life should apologise for our predecessors, and for the fact that the Legitimacy Act was passed in the Dáil in 1931. That this was the law of the land is horrendous.[88]

Banished and Abused Children of Eve

Thousands of children entered the austere setting of a residential industrial school, where harsh, rigid and abusive regimes persisted and where little or no private contact with family was permitted. Potential scrutiny by inspectors was 'stage-managed' by those in authority in the institution and colluded with by government representatives. Ferriter writes that inspectors from the Department of Education engaged in a 'deferential submissive attitude to the religious congregations' and failed 'to carry out meaningful inspections.'

In his research into 'The Report of the Commission to Inquire into Child Abuse' [also known as the Ryan Report], Ferriter states that it 'contains the testimony of hundreds of such victims' and that

> . . . thousands of children suffered systematic physical and sexual abuse between the 1930s and the 1970s and lived in a climate of fear in residential institutions funded by the state and run by religious orders.[89]

Ferriter continues:

> More than 1,700 men and women gave evidence of abuse
> to the Commission, chaired by Justice Seán Ryan, with
> over half reporting sexual abuse. The Commission's report
> details abuse in relation to 216 institutions, an extraordi-
> nary number for a country of Ireland's size. . . . The report
> found that sexual abuse was endemic in boys' institutions,
> and more allegations were made against the Christian
> Brothers, the largest provider of residential care for boys
> in the State, than all other male orders combined.[90]

Following examination of the content of the Ryan Report, Taoiseach Brian Cowen stated in the Dáil:

> That report . . . surely is one of the most important reports, and almost certainly the gravest, ever published in the history of the State. It contains a shattering litany of abuse of children in care in this country over many decades. In doing so it presents a searing indictment of the people who perpetrated that abuse, of the religious congregations who ran the institutions in which it took place, and of the organs of the State who failed in their duty to care for the children involved.[91]

Reflecting on the early twentieth century experience in the Irish Free State, there is a sense that the chaos that followed the administrative transition created a power vacuum. Into this power vacuum moved the authority of the Roman Catholic Church, with the general approval of government members. As poverty, desperation, the contagion of tuberculosis and emigration touched the lives of a large proportion of the population outside the walls of the institutions, within those walls, extreme controls were exercised on the most vulnerable women and children, while the same holders of power preached compliance from the pulpit to the struggling many.

Compliance with doctrine, patriarchal structures and Catholic Church activities were promoted and emphasised at times when the risk of social revolt and demands for improvement in welfare and employment supports seemed likely. While political upheaval was the norm in mainland Europe in the mid-1900s, McQuaid drew the attention of the populace to religious practice through attendance at Holy Year (1950) and Marian Year (1954) obligations. John Cooney comments:

So resurgent was the mood of popular piety in Dublin that a Jewish T.D., Robert Briscoe remarked, 'the more Catholic the people became the more he liked it'.[92]

McQuaid's desire to maintain the status quo was further evident in the management of the National Society for Prevention of Cruelty to Children (NSPCC). Ferriter refers to reports from the NSPCC during the 1940s and 1950s that

. . . graphically illustrate specific cases of neglect, squalor and parental irresponsibility, as well as calling for legal adoption, and strongly criticising the excessive use of industrial schools as an alternative to providing a new family life for the victims.[93]

The pleas of the NSPCC

. . . went unheard and in 1956, when Archbishop McQuaid assumed control of the society, challenging and graphic case studies went and awkward questions posed about adoption and industrial schools were jettisoned in favour of quaint, superficial stories with happy endings. There was no context and no challenge. The exposure of the underbelly had ground to a halt.[94]

Having assumed control of the society and the message, McQuaid asserted that the public 'have proven again that they are good guardians of the nation's conscience'; and the society's aim remained essentially conservative, focused on damage limitation – 'the primary function of our society is to ensure that the life of every child in the state shall at least be endurable'.[95]

Taoiseach Brian Cowen stated in the Dáil:

The historical survey contained in the [Ryan] report demonstrates how the industrial school system came to form part of the apparatus of social control, which, together with the effects of sustained emigration, came to be a primary response to the endemic problems of under-development, under-employment and poverty. As the report notes, against the background of extreme poverty, some saw schools as no worse than anything else and as offering children at least adequate food, clothing and housing.[96]

Does God see us?
God sees us, for nothing is hidden from
his all-seeing eye. (Hebrews 4:13) [97]

Turning Over the Truth and Toppling Those at the Top

Diarmaid Ferriter writes that:

> There is now no doubt that from the 1930s the Church authorities were aware of sexual abuse and had canon law structures in place to deal with it.[98]

> In July, 2004, Brother John O'Shea the regional leader of the Brothers of Charity, referred to an 'authoritarian atmosphere in schools and institutions which made even credible people afraid to complain' and noted that 'they were seen as a group rather than as individuals in a group'. He suggested, accurately, that sexual abuse was seen as a moral issue with the emphasis on the spiritual, 'and a focus on the celibate life of the accused rather than on the abuse and hurt caused'.[99]

Between 1930 and 1995, the Christian Brothers housed 10,000 children

> . . . in their residential institutions: up until 2004, 791 complaints of abuse had been made against the Brothers. The Sisters of Mercy had 2,522 children in their care in 1941, but each convent was autonomous; from 1940 until the closure of their institutions, the Good Shepherd Sisters looked after 1,735 children. In 2004 they would not admit or deny abuse had occurred, but maintained 'there is a grey area in between where we are not sure'.[100]

Does God know all things?
God knows all things, past, present and to come,
even our most secret thoughts and actions.[101]

Referring to the Ryan Report, Ferriter continues:

The report also makes it clear that the extent of the sexual and physical assaults on children cannot be explained
away by maintaining that the country was too poor and ig-
norant; there were much more calculated and sinister forces at work and a deliberate abdication of state responsibility... There was a casual indifference to everyday violence
that would not have been tolerated in other countries. The
children enduring the thrashings were mostly poor and
held in contempt, victims of an invidious Irish snobbery in
a country that liked to pretend it was classless.[102]

Many of the perpetrators of abuse were victims of another snobbery – the internal Church pecking order that deemed certain clerics to be more suited to working in industrial schools. There is no doubt that the frustrations they experienced had devastating consequences for the children and for themselves. They were products of a uniquely Irish mixture of large families, thwarted ambitions, rigorous segregation of the sexes and lack of economic opportunity, as were the children they took out their frustration on, often in the most sadistic of ways.[103]

'Is the Church infallible?
The Church is infallible, that is, it cannot err, when it teaches doctrines of faith and morals to be held by all the faithful.[104]

Taoiseach Brian Cowen stated in the Dáil:

> It is not only the Government that must reflect and act on the commission's report. The religious congregations face an important moral responsibility, which the Government and this House have made clear to them, to make further substantial contributions by way of reparation. It seems clear that how they meet that responsibility will deeply influence how the Irish people judge finally the extent to which the congregations live up to the values of their founders.[105]

> *Who in the Church can teach infallibily?*
> *The infallible teachers in the Church are the Pope,*
> *and the general body of the bishops united with the Pope.*[106]

Deference Dominates and Identity is Lost

The micro-management of parish and diocesan activities is illustrated in the following extract from *John Charles McQuaid*, in which Cooney writes:

> McQuaid kept his clergy on a tight rein and did not tolerate priests from other dioceses performing services and taking part in public meetings in Dublin without his permission.

Concerned that nuns holidaying in Ireland from England might bring with them negative influences, he and his fellow bishops approached their peers in England

> . . . to secure their cooperation in ensuring' that these visiting nuns stayed in 'a religious house of women' . . . and 'parish priests throughout Ireland were instructed to report to their bishops when any nuns were spotted holidaying in their areas'.[107]

As Taoiseach Brian Cowen stated in the Dáil:

> On behalf of the State and of all citizens of the State, the Government wishes to make a sincere and long overdue apology to the victims of childhood abuse for our collective failure to intervene, to detect their pain, to come to their rescue.[108]

More than a decade later Tánaiste Leo Varadkar stated:

> The survivors of the mother and baby institutions, alongside the survivors of industrial schools, constitute Ireland's stolen generation. As a society and as a State, we stole from them, their lives they should have had, raised by their mothers in their own communities, known to their fathers, brought up to believe they were as good as anyone else and could grow up to be anyone they wanted to be.[109]

McQuaid's efforts to maintain the image of Ireland as being 'a place apart' and 'free from sin' were tested when reports on adoption of Irish babies and toddlers began to appear in the newspapers. Diarmaid Ferriter writes:

In March 1950 *The New York Times* printed a photograph of six Irish children departing Shannon airport for adoption by US couples; 'press coverage reached a crisis in 1951 when newspapers in the United States, Britain and Ireland documented how easy it was for the actress Jane Russell to adopt an Irish national who was living in London with his parents'.

In 1945, Archbishop McQuaid had told Stephen Roche of the Department of Justice that 'no step be taken' until the Hierarchy was notified about any adoption legislation.[110]

McQuaid was concerned that social workers were escalating the matter of foreign adoptions and that unwanted attention was being drawn to the existing process.

The social workers, as far back as 1945, were reporting that 'there is far too much trading in babies at present amongst those who take them for a lump sum. Sometimes the child is sent from one woman to another, the sum getting smaller and smaller at each transfer. It is difficult to trace some of these children and they may suffer much hardship.[111]

The process of legislating on the question of adoption moved slowly over several years. The CIMBH report documented that:

Archbishop McQuaid and Fr Cecil Barrett [Head of the Catholic Social Welfare Bureau], who strictly speaking had no right to be involved at all, were actively involved in trying to control foreign adoptions and did manage to have some standards applied.[112]

Taoiseach Enda Kenny stated in the Dáil:

We lived with the damaging idea that what was desirable and acceptable in the eyes of the church and the State was the same and interchangeable.[113]

As John Cooney explains:

> The closed nature of Irish society enabled McQuaid to exploit a cloak and dagger atmosphere in which he could influence legislators. A classic example of McQuaid's political *modus operandi* was his vetting of proposed adoption legislation, the groundwork for which had been prepared by an episcopal committee under his chairmanship. McQuaid had deployed two Maynooth theologians to examine the issue with the parliamentary draftsman.[114]

Accordingly, on January 3, 1952, McQuaid handed the Minister for Justice, Gerald Boland, a memorandum which 'excellently solved' the 'very grave spiritual issues' governing the adoption of children. Once Boland nodded his consent, McQuaid announced that 'legal adoption, if it be restricted within certain limits and protected by certain safeguards, is consonant with Catholic teaching'.[115]

McQuaid's willingness to allow the State establish a legal framework for adoption, in 1952 was an advance on his opposition to such a move by Boland in 1944 and by the Inter-Party Minister for Health, General Seán MacEoin in 1950–51. A major factor in this shift was his desire to avoid a possible public scandal over the sending of illegitimate children to America… With the passage of the 1952 Act, McQuaid not only regularised American adoptions but also had the State endorse his sectarian approach.[116]

As Taoiseach Enda Kenny stated in the Dáil:

For 90 years Ireland subjected these women and their ex perience to a profound and studied indifference.[117]

What is despair?
Despair is the refusal to trust in God
for the graces necessary for salvation.[118]

The history of the evolution of adoption legislation in Ireland can be seen as a significant test in management of boundaries and message. Since the Irish Free State was established in 1922, the mindset of being 'a place apart' and chosen by God to be model citizens of the world was tested by media reports of desperate Irish girls and women in English ports and cities and again by the Jane Russell story and others, which reported on removal of children from Ireland for adoption elsewhere.

In some cases babies were bought – 'contributions' were made to the institutions that housed the babies, many of which were overcrowded at a time when births to unmarried mothers were on the increase – and for the prospective adopters the babies' removal was 'effortless acquisition', in contrast to Britain where adoption laws forbade such practices.[119]

It was during a period in Irish history when poverty, large families, high unemployment, a TB contagion and continuous emigration was the norm. Therefore, it is without question that many of the children who were taken from these shores found themselves in caring families and experienced a childhood and a lifestyle that could only have been dreamt of in Ireland.

However, as Ferriter documents,

... many grew to adulthood under assumed names and this 'created serious issues of confused identity when the truth

was revealed or found out, as did the fact that the mother's name was in some cases deleted from the record.' . . . The mothers had signed forms that included wording: 'I hereby relinquish full claim forever to my child' and authorisation for the children to be taken out of the country. Some who had spent nearly two years caring for their children were distraught, yet were forbidden to question the procedure.[120]

The report of the CIMBH states that:

> Many allegations have been made that large sums of money were given to the institutions and agencies in Ireland that arranged foreign adoptions. Such allegations are impossible to prove and impossible to disprove. One person who was adopted in the USA in the 1950s provided the Commission with documentary evidence of the costs of his adoption. They included an airfare of $273, and a payment of $142 to Sean Ross [Mother and Baby Home], which included a contribution to the cost of the airfare of the adult who accompanied the child on the flight. Further costs incurred included payments for a home study report [family assessment], medical reports and legal costs in finalising the adoption.[121]

Ferriter refers to the research of Mike Milotte:

> 2,100 children were sent to America under this scheme between 1949 and the end of 1973. Of the 330 foreign adoption cases in 1952, 327 were illegitimate children and 3 were orphans. There was no restriction on the entry of these children to the US, but the 'consent' of young and vulnerable Irish single mothers was in many cases no such thing.[122]

The report of the CIMBH states that:

> Institutional and official external records examined by the Commission [of Investigation into Mother and Baby Homes], show that 1,638 children who were resident in the mother and baby homes and county homes under investigation were placed for foreign adoption. The vast majority, 1,427 were placed for adoption in the United States of America. The report also states that 'The Adoption Act 1952 did not regulate foreign adoptions.'[123]

When is an oath lawful?
For an oath to be lawful we must have sufficient reason
for taking it, and we must say only what is true,
or promise only what is lawful.[124]

Change Creeps Slowly Over Closed Minds and Hearts

The report of the CIMBH states that:

> The delay in introducing legal adoption explains why many Irish women spent such a long time in mother and baby homes. When adoption became widespread in the 1960s the average length of stay fell significantly and continued to fall in the 1970s.[125]

The report continues:

> By the 1960s . . . 74 per cent of children leaving Sean Ross [mother and baby home] were adopted, and the number who were recorded as having left with their mother had fallen to 19 per cent compared with almost 66 per cent in the 1940s.[126]

> By the 1960s most women placed their child for adoption and left the mother and baby homes within a few months of giving birth. In 1967 the number of babies adopted was 97 per cent of the number of 'illegitimate' births. These statistics dispel any myth that the 1960s brought major changes in family or societal attitudes or practices towards illegitimacy.[127]

> The number of births to unmarried mothers doubled between 1971 and 1980. In 1980 a total of 552 babies were born to women who were in mother and baby homes. This figure was higher than the 498 born in these homes in 1950 or the 456 babies born in 1960. The numbers only began to fall in the 1980s. Mother and baby homes were closed, down-sized or were replaced by flatlets and hostels. In 1971, the number of adoption orders was 71 per cent of the number of 'illegitimate' births, by 1980 this had fallen to

37 per cent and to less than 9 per cent by 1990. By the late 1990s most adoption orders in Ireland were family adoptions, or adoptions of foreign-born children.[128]

There are many reasons behind the dramatic reduction in the numbers of Irish-born children placed for adoption in the closing decades of the twentieth century. Included were the changes taking place in civil society, such as the introduction of a social

welfare payment for single mothers, increased access to contraception, expansion of diverse views being debated in the media
and women and men of grit and courage speaking of their experiences of rejection and abuse on the national airwaves.

For unmarried mothers and their infants, the most important
shift in attitude came with the abolishment of the term 'illegitimate' when referring to children. Parallel to these processes was
the reluctant transition of power from Archbishop John Charles
McQuaid to Archbishop Dermot Ryan in 1972, followed a year
later by the sudden death of McQuaid.

Ferriter writes:

> On some levels, by the 1970s there was more of a willing-
> ness on the part of the Catholic Church and the medical
> profession to be less judgemental in their approach to
> young women and their pregnancies .

And following a key recommendation of the Commission on
the Status of Women

> . . . the introduction of a state allowance for unmarried
> mothers in 1973 was important in reducing the stigma.[129]

In addition, in 1974 Mary Robinson

> . . . first tabled a motion on the rights of illegitimate chil-
> dren' [and] largely as a result [of her efforts] the status of
> 'illegitimate' was legally abolished in 1987.[130]

However significant these changes were in legislation, the
day-to-day reality for most women in Ireland remained stagnant
and oppressive. The existence of a competition entitled *House-
wife of the Year*, which was broadcast on RTÉ between 1968 and
1995, speaks volumes about the rigidity of thinking regarding

the role of women in Irish society. The women were judged on their cookery, mothering and household management ability. The inclusion of the word 'wife' reinforced the values declared in Articles 41.1 and 41.2 of the Bunreacht na h'Éireann. These values assigned women's role and 'duties' as being entirely within the family home.

The 1980s Exercised Irish Minds

A number of disturbing events took place in the 1980s in the lives of Irish girls and women, ones which could no longer be silenced or contained by local and church authorities. Significant among these was the death of Ann Lovett in 1984, in a small town in County Longford. The troubling circumstances of her death opened the floodgates of revelations on previously taboo subjects in Irish society and exposed hypocrisy at many levels.

Ann was a fifteen-year-old school girl who died within hours of giving birth to a stillborn baby in a grotto. She lay there alone in her school uniform on wet stones, below a statue of the Blessed Virgin Mary and the kneeling Saint Bernadette, and gave birth to a boy. She then wrapped the infant in her coat and lay on the slab, weak and bleeding, on a cold, wet January day.

Ann's death and other outrages against women challenged the patriarchal structures imposed on generations of girls and women. The collective anger of Irish women and their supporters became overwhelming on the national airwaves and began to influence legislators in how they considered women's and children's rights. At the time, I was a few years older than Ann, and her death and the despair that consumed young women of the period added to my commitment to leave the country.

Also influential during those years were revelations that unveiled church hierarchy and clergy to be human and flawed like the general population. Most notably among these was the news in 1992 that Bishop Eamon Casey had a secret son. However, it was the content of the report of the 'Commission to Inquire into Child Abuse' and the work of journalist Mary Raftery and others which were to signal a toppling from power of the ordained men who knew about and sometimes participated directly or indirectly in the profound abuse of children over many decades.

During the Dáil Debate on the Report of the Commission of Investigation into Mother and Baby Homes, Deputy Holly Cairns stated:

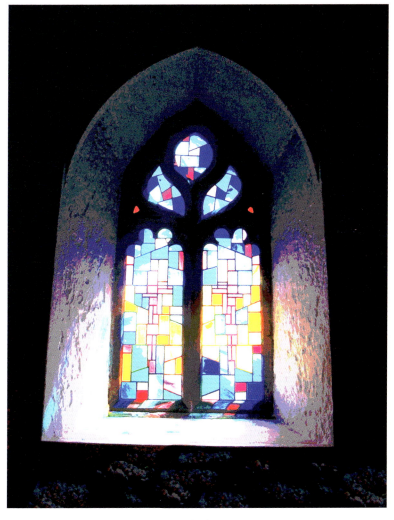

There are no words for this cascade of misogyny, abuse and criminality perpetuated against women and their children. The last thing the survivors need is inadequate apologies from more men in positions of power. They deserve justice, genuine contrition from church and State and complete and unreserved redress. The shame used to control and incarcerate women and children for the so-called crime of getting pregnant was endemic in our society and was misplaced. It is time we re-direct the shame to where it belongs. Shame on the people who committed these horrendous crimes, on the religious orders which oversaw it and on successive Governments for facilitating and condoning it.[131]

Banished Eve and Her Children: A Conclusion

The decades that followed the establishment of the Irish Free State proved to be a cold and harsh environment for many across this island and for those who, for diverse reasons, left these shores, often never to return. For many women and children the experience of repression, containment and silencing had a profoundly abusive impact and has burdened them with life-long scars. As citizens of this new Ireland, these scars collectively leave a legacy of shadow and shame. They inspire those of us who follow to be alert, active and resistant in the face of injustice and misogyny, which often remains hidden in plain sight, and ultimately no one benefits, no one thrives and families are fractured.

The voices of women and children who witnessed and endured the institutions into which they were born or admitted to are resounding in their depth of loss, rejection and emotional pain. To truly listen evokes waves of sadness and anger for what they suffered, and gratefulness that they survived, were willing to speak and found the courage to do so.

Those whose voices contributed to the numerous commissions of inquiry or investigations are documented within those pages and national broadcasts. Each deserves individual attention and respect. To elevate one from among the many would be to do disservice to them all. As a nation we owe them a depth of gratitude, honour and redress.

We must never forget and never attempt to extinguish or rewrite their experience from our local and cultural history and our records of the past. Their experience must be made visible in national monuments to Ireland's Stolen Generation and our children must be told what happened to girls, women and children in Ireland.

Collective anger or rage is also a natural function.
There is such a phenomenon as group hurt, group grief.
Women who become socially, politically, or culturally
conscious often find that they have to deal with
a collective rage that seeps upward through
them again and again.

It is psychically sound for women to feel this anger. It
is psychically sound for them to use this anger about
injustice to invent ways to elicit useful change. It is
not psychologically sound for them to neutralize their
anger so they will not feel, so they will therefore not
press for evolution and change.

As with personal rage, collective anger is also a teacher.
Women can consult with it, question it in solitude and
with others, and act upon their conclusions.

– Clarissa Pinkola Estés[132]

ENDNOTES

Chapter 1

1. Dooley, T. (2014) *The Decline and Fall of the Dukes of Leinster, 1872–1948*, Four Courts Press, p. 7

2. Ferriter, D. (2009) *Occasions of Sin*, Profile Books, p. 17

3. Ibid., p. 9

4. Kennedy, P. (Editor) (2004) *Motherhood in Ireland*, Chapter 13, Guilbride, A. 'Infanticide: The Crime of Motherhood', Mercier Press, p. 171 (Refers to the research of 'Inglis, T. (1987) *Moral Monopoly, The Catholic Church in Modern Irish Society*, Dublin: Gill and Macmillan)

5. www.pearsemuseum.ie

6. Ibid.

7. Ryle Dwyer, T. (1991) *Eamon de Valera*, Chapter 1, Poolbeg Press (1991) then, Paperview UK in association with the *Irish Independent* (2006), pp. 9–12.

8. Ibid.

9. Cooney, J. (1999) *John Charles McQuaid*, O'Brien Press, then Paperview UK in association with the *Irish Independent* (2006), pp. 7–10

10. Ibid., p. 13

11. Ibid.

12. Ibid., p. 14

13. Ibid., p. 16

14. Ibid.

15. Ibid., p. 19

16. Ibid.

17. Ibid.

18. Ibid., p. 16

19. Ibid., p. 18

20. Ibid., p. 20

21. Ibid., p. 21

22. Ibid.

23. Ibid.

24. Ibid., p. 22

25. Ibid., p. 355

26. Ibid., p. 23

27. Ibid., p. 26

28. Ibid., p. 28

29. Ibid., p. 29

30. Ibid., p. 32

31. www.museum.ie

32. 'The Report of the Commission of Investigation into Mother and Baby Homes' (2021) www.assets.gov.ie, Chapter 9, p. 12 (9.25)

33. Ibid., p. 12 (9.24)

34. Ibid., p. 13 (9.26)

35. Ibid., p. 14 (9.28) (Refers to research by K.H. Connell, *Irish Peasant Society: Four Historical Essays* (Oxford, 1968); *Catholicism and Marriage in the Century after the Famine*, pp. 113–161 and Timothy Guinnane, *The Vanishing Irish: Households, Migration, and the Rural Economy in Ireland*, 1850–1914 (Princeton, 1997), p. 218

36. Ibid., p. 11 (9.23)

37. Ibid., pp. 11-12 (9.23)

38. Ibid., p. 14 (9.28)

39. Ibid., Executive Summary, pp. 14-15 (46)

40. Ibid.

41. 'Irish Independent Eucharistic Congress Souvenir Number, 1932' (a quotation from a sermon by Most Rev. Dr McNamee, Bishop of Armagh, on 'The Struggle for the Faith'), p. 2.

42. Ibid., p. 16

43. Ibid., p. 2

44. Chesler, P. (2005) *Women and Madness*, Palgrave MacMillan, p. 160

45. Pinkola Estés, C. (1998) *Women Who Run with Wolves*, Random House, p. 176

Chapter 2

1. Kennedy, P. (Editor) (2004) *Motherhood in Ireland*, Chapter 13, Guilbride, A. 'Infanticide: The Crime of Motherhood', Mercier Press, p. 176

2. Ibid., p. 171

3. Ibid., pp. 172-173

4. Ibid., p. 173

5. Ibid. (With reference to Lyons J. B. (1980) *Oliver St John Gogarty: The Man of Many Talents*, Blackwater Press)

6. 'The Report of the Commission of Investigation into Mother and Baby Homes', www.assets.gov.ie, Chapter 4, p. 41 (4.97)

7. Kennedy, *Motherhood in Ireland*, Chapter 13, Guilbride, p. 173.

8. Ibid.

9. Ibid., pp. 173-174 (With reference to Jackson, P. Conroy (1987) 'Outside the Jurisdiction: Irish Women Seeking Abortion' in Smyth (ed) (1992) *The Abortion Papers*, Attic Press, pp. 119-137

10. Ferriter, D. (2009) *Occasions of Sin*, Profile Books, p. 119

11. 'The Report of the Commission of Investigation into Mother and Baby Homes', Chapter 4, p. 33 (4.80)

12. Ferriter, *Occasions of Sin*, pp. 101–102

13. Ibid., p. 127

14. 'The Report of the Commission of Investigation into Mother and Baby Homes', Chapter 4, p. 1 (4.3)

15. Ferriter, *Occasions of Sin*, p. 127

16. 'The Report of the Commission of Investigation into Mother and Baby Homes', Chapter 9, p. 44 (9.95).

17. Pinkola Estés, C. (1998) *Women Who Run With Wolves*, Random House, p. 175

Chapter 3

1. Kennedy, P. (Editor) (2004) *Motherhood in Ireland*, Chapter 10, Conroy, P. 'Maternity Confined: The Struggle for Fertility Control', p. 130 (With reference to the Commission on Emigration, 1955)

2. Kennedy, P. (Editor) (2004) *Motherhood in Ireland*, Chapter 13, Guilbride, A. 'Infanticide: The Crime of Motherhood', Mercier Press, p. 178

3. Ferriter, D. (2009) *Occasions of Sin*, Profile Books, p. 129

4. Ibid., p. 263

5. 'The Report of the Commission of Investigation into Mother and Baby Homes', www.assets.gov.ie, Chapter 9, pp. 6–7 (9.14)

6. Kennedy, *Motherhood in Ireland*, Chapter 13, Guilbride, A., p. 178

7. 'The Report of the Commission of Investigation into Mother and Baby Homes', Chapter 9, p. 20 (9.41)

8. Kennedy, *Motherhood in Ireland*, Chapter 10, Conroy, P., p. 130

9. Ferriter, *Occasions of Sin*, p. 282

10. Ibid., p. 279

11. 'The Report of the Commission of Investigation into Mother and Baby Homes', Chapter 9, p. 22 (9.43)

12. Ibid., Executive Summary, p. 14 (45)

13. Ferriter, *Occasions of Sin*, p. 283

14. Ibid., p. 278

15. Ibid., p. 279

16. Ibid.

17. Ibid.

18. Ibid., p. 280

19. Cooney, J. (1999) *John Charles McQuaid*, O'Brien Press, then Paperview UK Ltd in association with the *Irish Independent* (2006), p. 105

20. Ferriter, *Occasions of Sin*, p. 228

21. Ibid., pp. 279–280

22. 'The Report of the Commission of Investigation into Mother and Baby Homes', Chapter 9, p. 58 (9.122)

23. Ibid., pp. 57-58

24. Ibid., p. 59 (9.126)

25. Pinkola Estés, C. (1998) *Women Who Run With Wolves*, Random House, p 365

Chapter 4

1. www.museum.ie

2. Cooney, J. (1999) *John Charles McQuaid*, O'Brien Press, then Paperview UK in association with the *Irish Independent* (2006), p. 43

3. Kennedy, P. (Editor) (2004) *Motherhood in Ireland*, Chapter 13, Guilbride, A., 'Infanticide: The Crime of Motherhood' (With reference to Keogh, D. (1994) *Twentieth-century Ireland: Nation and State*, Gill & Macmillan), Mercier Press, p. 171

4. Ibid., p. 171

5. Cooney, *John Charles McQuaid*, p. 43

6. Ibid., p. 44

7. Ibid., p. 53

8. Ibid., p. 46

9. Ibid., pp. 68–69

10. Kennedy, *Motherhood in Ireland*, Chapter 10, Conroy, P. 'Maternity Confined: The Struggle for Fertility Control', pp. 128–129

11. Ibid., p. 128

12. Cooney, *John Charles McQuaid*, p. 75

13. Ibid., p. 84

14. Ibid., p. 79

15. Kennedy, *Motherhood in Ireland*, Chapter 10, Conroy, P., p. 129

16. Kennedy, *Motherhood in Ireland*, Chapter 13, Guilbride, pp. 177–178

17. Kennedy, *Motherhood in Ireland*, Chapter 10, Conroy, pp. 130–131

18. Kennedy, *Motherhood in Ireland*, Chapter 11, Hilliard, B., 'Motherhood, Sexuality and the Catholic Church', p. 147

19. Ibid., p. 139

20. Ibid., p. 146

21. Ibid., p. 147

22. Ibid., p. 148

23. Ibid., pp. 148-149

24. Rich, A. (1976) *Of Woman Born*, Virago, p. 57

25. Chesler, P. (2005) *Women and Madness*, Palgrave MacMillan, p. 44.

Chapter 5

1. Ferriter, D. (2009) *Occasions of Sin*, Profile Books, p. 293

2. Cooney, J. (1999) *John Charles McQuaid*, O'Brien Press, then Paperview UK in association with the *Irish Independent* (2006), p. 177

3. Ibid., p. 178

4. Ibid., p. 177

5. Ferriter, *Occasions of Sin*, p. 325

6. Rich, A. (1976) *Of Woman Born*, Virago, p. 61

7. Ferriter, *Occasions of Sin*, p. 346

8. Cooney, *John Charles McQuaid*, p. 305

Chapter 6

1. Pinkola Estés, C. (1998) *Women Who Run With Wolves*, Random House, p. 3

2   *A Catechism of Catholic Doctrine* (1951) Approved by the Archbishops and Bishops of Ireland, Imprimatur; Joannes Carolus Archiepiscopus Dublinensis, Gill & Son, p. 22 (54)

3. Ibid., p. 54 (206)

4. Varadkar, L. (2021) extract of statement made during 'Dáil debate on The Report of the Commission of Investigation into Mother and Baby Homes' (13 Jan 2021) www.oireachtas.ie

5. *A Catechism of Catholic Doctrine*, p. 23 (59)

6. Kennedy, P. (Editor) (2004) *Motherhood in Ireland*, Chapter 12, Burke Brogan, P. 'The Magdalene Experience', Mercier Press, p. 161

7. Varadkar, L., extract of statement made during 'Dáil debate on The Report of the Commission of Investigation into Mother and Baby Homes'

8   *A Catechism of Catholic Doctrine*, p. 62 (255)

9. Kenny, E. (2013) extract from statement made during 'Dáil debate on the Report of the Interdepartmental Committee to establish the facts of State involvement with the Magdalen laundries' (19 Feb 2013) www.oireachtas.ie

10. Ferriter, D. (2009) *Occasions of Sin*, Profile Books, p. 284

11. Edelman, H. (1996) *Motherless Daughters: The Legacy of Loss*, Hodder & Stoughton, p. 114

12. Ibid., pp, 82-83

13. *A Catechism of Catholic Doctrine*, p. 65 (273)

14. 'The Report of the Commission of Investigation into Mother and Baby Homes' (2021) www.assets.gov.ie, Executive Summary, p. 15 (48)

15. Ibid., p. 17 (50)

16. Ibid., Chapter 9, p. 21 (9.42)

17. Ibid., Executive Summary, p. 13 (43)

18. Ibid., p. 5 (16)

19. Martin, M. (2021) extract of statement made during 'Dáil debate on The Report of the Commission of Investigation into Mother and Baby Homes' (13 Jan 2021) www.oireachtas.ie

20. Ferriter, *Occasions of Sin*, p. 133

21. 'The Report of the Commission of Investigation into Mother and Baby Homes', Chapter 9, p. 36 (9.76)

22. Ibid., p. 37 (9.77)

23. 'Report of the Interdepartmental Committee to establish the facts of State Involvement with the Magdalen Laundries', (2013) www.assets.gov.ie., Chapter 9, p. 207 (5)

24. Ferriter, *Occasions of Sin*, p. 329 (Referencing research by Moira Maguire, 'The Carrigan Committee and Child Sexual Abuse in Twentieth-century Ireland', *New Hibernia Review*, vol. 11, no. 2, Summer 2007, pp. 79–101)

25. *A Catechism of Catholic Doctrine*, p. 65 (269)

26. Ibid., p. 60 (238)

27. 'The Report of the Commission of Investigation into Mother and Baby Homes', Executive Summary, p. 3 (8)

28. 'Report of the Interdepartmental Committee to establish the facts of State involvement with the Magdalene laundries', Chapter 8, p. 176 (46)

29. 'The Report of the Commission of Investigation into Mother and Baby Homes', Executive Summary, p. 47 (182)

30. Ibid., p. 3 (9)

31. Ibid., p. 2 (1)

32. Ibid.

33. Edelman, *Motherless Daughters: The Legacy of Loss*, pp. 75–76

34. *A Catechism of Catholic Doctrine*, p. 23 (60)

35. 'The Report of the Commission of Investigation into Mother and Baby Homes', Chapter 9, p. 25 (9.49)

36. Ferriter, *Occasions of Sin*, pp. 328–329

37. Ibid., p. 329

38. 'The Report of the Commission of Investigation into Mother and Baby Homes', Executive Summary, p. 2 (2)

39. Ibid., p. 17 (51)

40. *A Catechism of Catholic Doctrine*, p. 23 (62)

41. Edelman, *Motherless Daughters: The Legacy of Loss*, pp. 200–201

42. *A Catechism of Catholic Doctrine*, p. 57 (230)

43. 'The Report of the Commission of Investigation into Mother and Baby Homes', Executive Summary, p. 63 (226)

44. Ibid.

45. *A Catechism of Catholic Doctrine*, p. 18 (31)

46. 'Report of the Interdepartmental Committee to establish the facts of State involvement with the Magdalen laundries', Chapter 19, p. 951 (52)

47. Ibid., p. 931 (28)

48. Ibid.

49. Ibid., p. 932 (31)

50. *A Catechism of Catholic Doctrine*, p. 65 (274)

51. 'The Report of the Commission of Investigation into Mother and Baby Homes', Executive Summary, p. 15 (48)

52. 'Report of the Interdepartmental Committee to establish the facts of State involvement with the Magdalen laundries', Chapter 19, p. 960 (67)

53. Chesler, P. (2005) *Women and Madness*, Palgrave Macmillan (With Reference to Margaret Fuller, 'The Great Lawsuit. Man versus Men. Woman versus Women,' *The Dial*, July 1843. Reprinted in *Margaret Fuller, American Romantic: A Selection from Her Writings and Correspondence* (1963), edited by Perry Miller, Cornell University Press), p. 291

54. 'The Report of the Commission of Investigation into Mother and Baby Homes', Executive Summary, p. 48 (183)

55. Gardner F. (2004) 'To enliven her was my living', *British Journal of Psychotherapy*, 21(1) 2004, pp. 49–62 (With reference to *Winnicott* Phillips, A., Fontana, 1988, p. 29)

56. 'The Report of the Commission of Investigation into Mother and Baby Homes', Executive Summary, p. 50 (191)

57. Ibid., p. 50 (192)

58. *A Catechism of Catholic Doctrine*, p. 69 (291)

59. Ferriter, D. (2005) *The Transformation of Ireland, 1900–2000*, Profile Books, p. 395

60. Ibid.

61. Ibid.

62. Ibid., p. 395-396

63. Ibid., p. 395

64. Cooney, J. (1999) *John Charles McQuaid*, O'Brien Press, then Paperview UK Ltd in association with the *Irish Independent* (2006), p. 112

65. Ibid., pp. 113

66. Ibid., p. 114

67. Ferriter, *The Transformation of Ireland*, p. 396

68. *A Catechism of Catholic Doctrine*, p. 69 (295)

69. 'The Report of the Commission of Investigation into Mother and Baby Homes', Executive Summary, p. 61 (222)

70. 'Report of the Interdepartmental Committee to establish the facts of State involvement with the Magdalen laundries', Chapter 17, p. 836 (70)

71. 'The Report of the Commission of Investigation into Mother and Baby Homes', Executive Summary, p. 64 (230)

72. Ibid., pp. 21–22 (62)

73. O'Gorman, R. (2021) extract of statement made during 'Dáil debate on The report of the Commission of Investigation into Mother and Baby Homes' (13 Jan 2021) www.oireachtas.ie

74. *A Catechism of Catholic Doctrine*, p. 31 (99)

75. 'The Report of the Commission of Investigation into Mother and Baby Homes', Executive Summary, p. 63-64 (229)

76. Ibid., p. 22 (63)

77. Ibid.

78. *A Catechism of Catholic Doctrine*, p. 31 (100)

79. 'The Report of the Commission of Investigation into Mother and Baby Homes', Executive Summary, p. 66 (239)

80. Martin, M. (2021) extract of statement made during 'Dáil debate on the report of the Commission of Investigation into Mother and Baby Homes'

81. Bysshe Shelley, P. (1818) (extract from) 'Stanzas Written in Dejection, near Naples', *Soundings: Poems We Did for Our Leaving Cert* edited by Augustine Martin (2010) Gill and Macmillan, p. 116

82. 'The Report of the Commission of Investigation into Mother and Baby Homes', Chapter 9, p. 59 (9.126)

83. *A Catechism of Catholic Doctrine*, p. 22 (56)

84. Martin, M. (2021) extract of statement made during 'Dáil debate on the report of the Commission of Investigation into Mother and Baby Homes'

85. 'The Report of the Commission of Investigation into Mother and Baby Homes', Chapter 9, p. 46 (9.99)

86. Ibid., p. 50 (9.104)

87. Cooney, *John Charles McQuaid*, p. 241

88. Kelly, A. (2021) extract from statement made during 'Dáil debate on the report of the Commission of Investigation into Mother and Baby Homes' (13 Jan 2021) www.oireachtas.ie.

89. Ferriter, D., *Occasions of Sin*, pp. 332–333

90. Ibid., p. 333

91. Cowen, B (2009) extract from 'Dáil statement on the Report of the Commission to Inquire into Child Abuse' (aka 'The Ryan Report') (11 June 2009) www.oireachtas.ie

92. Cooney, *John Charles McQuaid*, p. 173

93. Ferriter, *Occasions of Sin*, p. 324

94. Ibid.

95. Ibid.

96. Cowen, B (2009) extract from 'Dáil statement on the Report of the Commission to Inquire into Child Abuse' (aka 'The Ryan Report')

97. *A Catechism of Catholic Doctrine*, p. 15 (8)

98. Ferriter, *Occasions of Sin*, p. 326

99. Ibid.

100. Ibid

101. *A Catechism of Catholic Doctrine*, p. 15 (9)

102. Ferriter, *Occasions of Sin*, p. 333

103. Ibid., pp. 333-334

104. *A Catechism of Catholic Doctrine*, p. 42 (158)

105. Cowen, B (2009) extract from 'Dáil statement on the Report of the Commission to Inquire into Child Abuse' (aka 'The Ryan Report')

106. *A Catechism of Catholic Doctrine*, p. 43 (160)

107. Cooney, *John Charles McQuaid*, p. 216

108. Cowen, B (2009) extract from 'Dáil statement on the Report of the Commission to Inquire into Child Abuse' (aka 'The Ryan Report')

109. Varadkar, L. (2021) extract of statement made during 'Dáil debate on the report of the Commission of Investigation into Mother and Baby Homes'

110. Ferriter, *Occasions of Sin*, p. 330

111. Ibid., pp 330-331

112. 'The Report of the Commission of Investigation into Mother and Baby Homes', Executive Summary, p. 72 (256)

113. Kenny, E. (2013) extract from statement made during 'Dáil debate on the Report of the Interdepartmental Committee to establish the facts of State involvement with the Magdalen laundries' (19 February 2013)

114. Cooney, *John Charles McQuaid*, pp. 220

115. Ibid.

116. Ibid., pp. 220-221

117. Kenny, E. (2013) extract from statement made during 'Dáil debate on the Report of the Interdepartmental Committee to establish the facts of State involvement with the Magdalen laundries'

118. *A Catechism of Catholic Doctrine*, p. 53 (203)

119. Ferriter, *Occasions of Sin*, pp. 331-332 (With reference to research by Mike Milotte (1997), *Banished Babies: The Secret History of Ireland's Baby Export Business*, New Island Books)

120. Ibid.

121. 'The Report of the Commission of Investigation into Mother and Baby Homes', Executive Summary, p. 73 (257)

122. Ferriter, *Occasions of Sin*, p. 331

123. 'The Report of the Commission of Investigation into Mother and Baby Homes', Executive Summary, p. 72 (255)

124 *A Catechism of Catholic Doctrine*, p. 56 (221)

125 'The Report of the Commission of Investigation into Mother and Baby Homes', Executive Summary, p. 50 (190)

126 Ibid., p. 55 (206)

127 Ibid., p. 22 (64)

128 Ibid., pp. 23-24 (67)

129 Ferriter, *Occasions of Sin*, pp. 437

130 Ibid., p. 524

131 Cairns, H. (2021) extract from statement made during 'Dáil debate on the report of the Commission of Investigation into Mother and Baby Homes' (13 Jan 2021) www.oireachtas.ie.

132 Pinkola Estés, C. (1998) *Women Who Run With Wolves*, Random House, p. 367

Listing of Photographs and Images

Except as otherwise noted, all photographs were taken by the author (all rights reserved). A number of photographs feature a collage of religious items and other objects chosen to symbolise the lived experience of women in Ireland between 1922 and 1972. Also, please note that:

- Some photographs featuring religious objects were taken in graveyards or grottos.

- Some photographs of a nun or a priest feature models.

- Photographs of most infants in a wicker basket or pram or in someone's arms feature dolls.

- There are some photographs of interiors, furniture, street views and buildings. The majority of these were taken at Bunratty Folk Park, County Clare.

- In all of the photographs taken by the author, artistic interpretation may be evident.

Listings by Page Number

Page 60 – A view of buildings through an archway at St. Patrick's Pontifical University, Maynooth, County Kildare.

Page 76 – A view of the convent in Kilcock, County Kildare.

Page 78 – Sacred Heart of Jesus (antique print) (edited)

Page 85 – Statue of the Immaculate Conception (The Virgin Mary) at the grotto on the grounds of Sean Ross Abbey (former Mother and Baby Home), Roscrea, County Tipperary.

Page 87 – Graveyard entrance on the grounds of St. Patrick's Pontifical University, Maynooth, County Kildare.

Page 99 – Buildings on the grounds of Sean Ross Abbey (former Mother and Baby Home), Roscrea, County Tipperary.

Page 100 – Advertisement from *Picturegoer* magazine, week ending June 4, 1949 (edited) page 76

Page 112 – A building at St. Patrick's Pontifical University, Maynooth, County Kildare.

Page 114 – Close-up view of the gate at a graveyard on the grounds of St. Patrick's Pontifical University, Maynooth, County Kildare.

Page 115 – Christian Brothers grave site, County Kildare

Page 117 – A building on the grounds of Sean Ross Abbey (former Mother and Baby Home), Roscrea, County Tipperary.

Page 122 – Nuns' graveyard, County Kildare.

Page 125 – Buildings on the grounds of Sean Ross Abbey (former Mother and Baby Home), Roscrea, County Tipperary.

Page 126 – Archbishop John Charles McQuaid and priest (author family archive)

Page 127 – Ration books from Ireland's Emergency Years.

Page 129 – A memorial at the children's grave site near the location of Tuam Mother and Baby Home, County Galway (artistic interpretation).